The Custom Dollhouse

The Complete Guide to Choosing, Decorating, Remodeling & Expanding Your Dollhouse

Nola Theiss

A Sterling/Lark Book
Sterling Publishing Co., Inc.   New York

Editor: Carol Taylor
Design: Marcia Winters, Sandra Montgomery
Production: Sandra Montgomery, Elaine Thompson

Library of Congress Cataloging in Publication Data
Theiss, Nola.
  The custom dollhouse : the complete guide to choosing,
decorating, remodeling & expanding your dollhouse / Nola
Theiss.
    p.   cm.
  "A Sterling/Lark book."
  Includes bibliographical references and index.
  Summary: A guide to choosing, decorating, remodeling,
and expanding dollhouses.
  ISBN 0-8069-8368-X
  1. Dollhouses.   [1. Dollhouses.]   I. Title.
TT175.3.T47   1991
745.592'3–dc20   91-12170
                                                       CIP
                                                        AC

ISBN 0-8069-8368-X

10 9 8 7 6 5 4 3 2 1

A Sterling/Lark Book

Produced by Altamont Press, Inc.
50 College St., Asheville, NC 28801

Published in 1991 by Sterling Publishing Co., Inc.
387 Park Ave. S., New York, NY 10016

Distributed in Canada by Sterling Publishing,
c/o Canadian Manda Group, P.O. Box 920,
    Station U, Toronto, Ontario M8Z 5P9
Distributed in the United Kingdom by Cassell PLC,
    Villiers House, 41/47 Strand, London WC2N 5JE, England
Distributed in Australia by Capricorn, Ltd., P.O. Box 665,
    Lane Cove, NSW 2066

Printed in Hong Kong

ACKNOWLEDGEMENTS

During the completion of this book, I called upon many dollhouse and components manufacturers and distributors of dollhouse furniture, wallpaper, flooring, tools and electrical kits. They were most generous in providing kits and materials, as well as advice, photography and artwork. They invited me to seminars, spent a great deal of time answering questions and showed faith that I would help the average person make the best decisions based on his or her own needs and abilities.

I would like to thank a number of these people personally: Connie Dixon, of Aztec Imports, a natural-born organizer, who introduced me to a number of products and sources and helped me decorate four houses; Jim Abrams, of Real Good Toys, whose innovative design elements in dollhouse construction have made assembly of quality dollhouses available to everyone; Lorraine Halaby and Harry Walmer, of Walmer dollhouses, a father-daughter team who produce classic quality dollhouses at many cost levels; Nancy Oriol, of Northeastern Scale Models, who provided a variety of wood moldings, trim and planks for me to try; Vern Skare of Cir-Kit Concepts, who has helped turn me into an electrical genius; Harry Candullo, of Houseworks, who made me feel like a kid at Christmas when he showed me all the possibilities of windows, doors, bookcases and fireplaces that can individualize a standard kit; and Hank Rosenthal, of Minigraphics who, in a few words, made me see interior decorating of a dollhouse as a work of art rather than the furnishing of individual rooms. I would also like to thank Excel Tools for their selection of miniature tools. Thanks also to Jessica Henry and Kathy Garner for sharing their dollhouse collections and ideas with me.

My husband Hal and daughters Elizabeth and Joanna gave their advice and forbearance as I turned my house and office into a dollhouse workshop and them into unpaid elves. I also want to thank my cousin Tony Ilchena who got me over my fear of electricity, and my coworkers Terry Zalenski and Diane Murphy, who lent their own dollhouse-building and instruction-writing experience to this book.

TABLE OF CONTENTS

INTRODUCTION

Like most hobbies, building a dollhouse makes no sense. No one has the extra time or the extra money to spare for something which has no direct use or purpose. Yet thousands of people build and enjoy dollhouses every year. Analyzing the excuses you've made to explain why you want one will help determine the best one to make.

I WANT TO MAKE A DOLLHOUSE FOR MY DAUGHTER.

This is the best excuse, because you can feel generous and self-sacrificing, but it isn't a valid one. Most girls are not old enough to help build a dollhouse or really appreciate the effort it takes until they reach an age when they are too cool to

play with either you or the dollhouse. This is the age between real childhood and second childhood, which is what people will say you are in.

When I was first bitten by the dollhouse bug, my daughters provided me with my excuse. Since I had two daughters, I figured I was entitled to two dollhouses. The first was the least expensive, preassembled-shell, quarter-inch-plywood model I could find. In one afternoon, we put in windows, doors and the staircase, and painted it. My six-year-old daughter decorated the house with leftover wallpaper and filled it with plastic furniture and small bears. She would not tolerate my interfering with her dollhouse anymore (except for buying occasional accoutrements as birthday gifts), because it served its purpose perfectly as a setting for her imagination. It also served my purpose, which was to find out whether I enjoyed working with a dollhouse and whether I was satisfied with a basic house. Unfortunately, the answers were yes and no, in that order.

I WANT TO MAKE A DOLLHOUSE BECAUSE I DON'T HAVE A DAUGHTER.

Many mothers of sons have realized that one of the reasons they wanted a daughter was that they don't enjoy playing with a boy's toys. Even in a nonsexist world of child raising, most parents won't buy their boy a dollhouse, so

many women buy one for themselves as compensation.

I WANT A DOLLHOUSE BECAUSE I HAVE SUCH FOND MEMORIES OF THE ONE I HAD IN MY CHILDHOOD.

Now, of course, you can have an even better one, because you are mature, skilled and have a bigger allowance.

I WANT A DOLLHOUSE BECAUSE I DIDN'T HAVE ONE WHEN I WAS A CHILD.

Well, now you can have one, because you are mature, skilled and have a bigger allowance. Besides, you always deserved one.

I WANT TO DESIGN, BUILD, DECORATE AND OWN A BEAUTIFUL HOUSE IN MINIATURE BECAUSE I CAN'T HAVE IT IN REALITY.

As expensive and time-consuming as dollhouses are, they are easy to build, cheap to decorate, and take little time, compared to a full-scale house. Besides, you don't have to worry about prevailing interest rates and mortgages, or live with plaster dust and a half-finished kitchen for months.

For those of us who live in a modern house, an old Victorian farmhouse, with its elaborate moldings and gingerbread trim, can be very comforting. As a fan of renovation shows and books, I enjoy applying some of the techniques I've learned on a little house rather than a full-scale project.

I WANT TO DESIGN, BUILD, DECORATE AND OWN A BEAUTIFUL HOUSE IN MINIATURE BECAUSE I AM A DESIGNER, BUILDER OR DECORATOR IN REALITY AND WANT TO HAVE A DOLLHOUSE AS A COMPLEMENT TO MY REAL HOUSE.

Applying our real-life skills to a fantasy can be as satisfying as using them for something practical. While you can't live in a dollhouse, it is a fascinating accessory in any decorating scheme.

If you really want to make a dollhouse, there are more than enough reasons to do it, but they all amount to the same thing: you want a dollhouse. The real question is whether you want the pleasure of the process or the pleasure of the finished project or both. You also need to know what level your skills are, how much you are willing to learn, how much time you have and how much money you want to spend initially. (Dollhouses are economic black holes: all spare change tends to disappear into them for decorating, furniture, electricity, etc., never to be seen again.)

The following chapters will help you decide which type of dollhouse is right for you by exploring the many aspects of style and size, the number of rooms, the question of expandability, the location of openings (back, front or combination), the level of realism and detail required, the quality of materials and the expense.

·*1*·

THE PERFECT DOLLHOUSE

Dollhouses are a lot like babies. When they belong to someone else, they are beautiful, fun to play with and easy to admire. When they are yours, they are difficult to raise, more work than you ever expected, very expensive, and never perfect or finished. Like your own children, dollhouses can give you huge amounts of satisfaction from participating in their growth and trying to shape them to our own image, and can drive you crazy as you realize your own shortcomings. They can also teach you skills you never knew you had. Babies and dollhouses require a long-term commitment—neither gets finished very quickly and both will be continuing drains on your resources. But, in both cases, often the more time, money and energy you invest, the better the finished result.

Fortunately, we get to choose what kind of dollhouse we want to build. The first decision is scale. Most dollhouses, furniture and accessories are built on a 1" to 1' scale. There are also kits made 1/2" to 1' scale, but even the 1" scale is barely workable for most adult-size hands, and there are other ways to drive yourself crazy.

BUILDING FROM SCRATCH

After you decide on the scale of your house, you must decide if you want to build from scratch or from a kit. Purists will want to design their own house, buy their own materials and produce their own individual creation. The advantages are obvious. You can imitate the style of your own abode, build your dream house or let your imagination go wild. Building a dollhouse without a kit requires drafting skills, plans and a workroom of power tools. There are a number of plan books available for craftspeople who want to build their own dollhouse without a kit but need some guidance. For most of us, dollhouse kits are complicated enough to keep us involved for a long time. Building from scratch is probably a project to undertake after a few kits have been built and you are ready for a greater challenge or to turn professional.

DOLLHOUSE KITS

Kits are usually priced according to the thickness of the plywood used, the amount of detail and styling, the amount of preassembly of the components and the authenticity of the details. Just checking the weight of a kit will give you a clue as to its price. Since plywood is the usual medium of dollhouse construction, its thickness is one sure sign of the price of a kit. Dollhouse kits can be classified into three main catagories: toys, the happy medium, and collector dollhouses.

DOLLHOUSE TOYS

The cheapest kits are made of 1/8" plywood or even heavy fiberboard. These kits usually are assembled with slots and tabs.

Many of these kits are very well designed with a choice of architectural styles and interesting details. While they will usually withstand the play of a child, the basic building materials are rather flimsy and the slot-and-tab assembly is not very sturdy. In

Some kits come with precut grooves, so that the pieces fit together smoothly and well. Assembly is relatively quick and easy.

general, these dollhouses are toys; by the time your child has outgrown them, they will be ready to be trashed. But they are relatively inexpensive: between $40 and $100 (£25–£60) for a kit, about the cost of a good pair of shoes.

THE HAPPY MEDIUM

In the moderate range are dollhouses usually made of 1/4" ply-

wood. Some come partially pre-assembled. Some have simulated siding worked into the basic plywood. Some come with precut grooves, so that the pieces slide together and fit in place before they are glued. They are assembled in a matter of minutes or hours, and after the glue has dried, they are ready for painting and decorating. They can literally be assembled on Christmas

Eve. These are good choices for the person who is interested primarily in decorating and finishing a dollhouse rather than building one.

When this type of dollhouse was first introduced, there were only a few choices of architectural style, but now there are many styles and many porches, side extensions, gazebos, etc., to individualize each house. These kinds of kits usually include non-working windows, a front door, stairs but no railings (except perhaps for a solid piece of wood to outline the stairs) and perhaps some trim. Often the railings or even the stairs will have to be assembled by you. Finishing kits or separate components such as shingles, clapboard siding, trim and shutters are available separately. The finished kits are usually about 16" to 18" deep, 24" to 26" wide and 26" to 30" high.

COLLECTOR DOLLHOUSES

The term "collector dollhouse" is used to describe a dollhouse made of 1/4" to 3/8" cabinet grade plywood. These are dollhouses meant for the serious miniature collector or the person who intends to build and decorate one dollhouse for the rest of his or her life or until he or she "needs" another one.

Their very size makes them special. Depending on the style, they measure 20" to 24" deep, 32" to 38" wide and 28" to 43" tall. The kits alone weigh 30 to 60 pounds. They have four to ten rooms, including bathrooms and hallways, and there are many extension kits available if you absolutely must have a greenhouse, an atrium, a room

Top: A plastic dollhouse toy. Bottom: A "happy medium" house.

for Grandma, a playroom for the kids, a deck or a gazebo. These kits have a range in price equivalent to that of a color television.

ber of rooms, the detail of the trim and what is included in the basic kit.

The usual components that come with a collector kit are

Collector dollhouse kits come in a wide variety of styles. With additions, sidings, trim, and paint, each can be "remodeled" into a completely unique house.

doors, nonworking windows, stairs, turned banisters and railings. In these quality kits, the scale is absolutely correct, the doors and windows look authentic, and the overall impression, even before the house is decorated, is that this is a miniature house, inside and out, not a toy.

DECIDING ON A DOLLHOUSE

Dollhouses made of lesser-quality materials may be fine if your purpose is to practice or to make a plaything for a child. The techniques and suggestions in this book apply equally well to less expensive models, but if you are going to spend as much time and effort as even a cheap dollhouse requires, you should wait until you can afford quality.

Ultimately, the basic quality of the materials is going to determine the quality of the finished work. I compare making a cheap dollhouse to knitting a sweater with poor-quality yarn. If you are going to spend the time making it, it had better look good and hold up for a long time, and not disappoint you by being unable to withstand wear and tear.

Take your time choosing the style, brand and size house because each of these factors has advantages and disadvantages. Buy the best kit you can afford. Go to miniature shows to get an overall view of what is available in your area. Subscribe to a miniature magazine and you will get on everyone's mailing list. Read and compare before you make a decision.

If you have a shop in your area which specializes in dollhouses, go in and pick the owner's brain. Most dollhouse shop owners are certifiably nuts about dollhouses and will be glad to share their enthusiasm and knowledge with you, but they will also have definite opinions which may or may not be right for you.

Ask to see a copy of the instructions for all the models you are considering. While all instructions will look complicated, you may find that some are easier to understand than others. Some may have more photographs and drawings that will help, as well. You will also be able to tell how many components have been preassembled and how much you will be expected to do. You may prefer to build your stairways riser by riser, or you may feel that it is worth paying a little more to get them preassembled. Don't expect the instructions to make complete sense in the store, where you are unable to unwrap and handle the actual pieces, but do look for basic clarity and directions you can follow.

Dollhouse store owners may be able to give you the names of people who sell assembled shells or completely decorated houses in your area. Often people will buy a dollhouse kit and hire someone to make it so they can give it as a gift. These professional builders are great sources of information about the ease of building and the quality of the different kits, since they have built so many. You may even want them to build the shell so you can do the decorating yourself. If you hire someone to build a dollhouse, expect to pay at least double the cost of the kit, depending on how complicated

Some extension kits can serve as either extensions or free-standing buildings. The gazebo-shaped portion of the porch above can stand on its own.

the job. Getting a bid may persuade you to build it yourself.

Often stores or professional builders offer workshops and classes on dollhouse building and decorating. Check your listing of local adult education classes for a dollhouse course in assembly, decorating or electrification. Take a course before you choose your kit if you possibly can. If all else fails, read through this book.

DECIDING FACTORS

After you pick everyone's brain, you will realize that choosing a dollhouse is a lot like choosing a real house. You need to know your price range, the architectural style you prefer, how many rooms you require, the quality of the basic materials, the luxuries you must have and those you can live without. You will want to know where and how you can expand later and whether this is a starter house or a dream house. You must also take into consideration the level of competence and the amount of time the builder has. Even location is important: you must have enough room to build and a place to leave your materials where they won't be disturbed. At least you don't have to worry about zoning.

PRICE

You should buy the best quality house you can afford, but there is considerable overlap between the highest price models of the moderate level houses and the lowest prices of the collector houses. The priciest moderate level houses will have more rooms, but the cheapest collec-tor houses will have more detail. Many of the components which may not be satisfactory in a moderate level house can be replaced later by more realistic materials, such as replacing solid banisters with turned railings or nonworking windows with working ones.

NUMBER OF ROOMS

The number of rooms you require is a totally personal decision. When I was buying my first collector house, I wouldn't consider a model without a bathroom because I wanted to buy miniature bathroom fixtures. A house didn't seem complete without a bathroom. Remember that you will have to furnish every room you have, which can be very expensive. For some people, decorating and furnishing are the most interesting parts of building a house and, of course, rooms can be sparsely furnished with pieces collected over the years.

Most manufacturers make dollhouse extensions so you can easily expand later, but adding these rooms will be more expensive than buying a bigger house in the first place. However, they can add interesting lines to a house, perhaps changing it from a basic rectangle to a many-winged mansion. Just as with a real house, adding on requires a certain amount of remodeling, but that too can add interest.

QUALITY OF MATERIALS

The quality of the materials makes all the difference in the final result. It is almost guaranteed that you will make a mistake somewhere along the line and will need to pull pieces apart or get replacement parts. It's amazing how perfectly sensible people will glue a wall with a cut-out door flat against another wall, or will cut through electrical tape when trimming wallpaper due to that "I'm really tired, but I'll just do one more thing before I quit" syndrome. Reputable manufacturers of quality dollhouses will sell you these replacement parts, since the success of the finished house is almost as important to them as it is to you. Every dollhouse is an advertisement for, or warning against, their company. Good, solid wood can withstand a little demolition work, and it will probably have to. The cheaper kits work fine if you don't make many mistakes.

DREAM HOUSE OR STARTER HOUSE?

You must also consider whether this is your dream house or a starter house. Buying a moderately priced starter house to make for a child as a trial run is a very good idea, if you can afford it. You will have the opportunity to learn the basic building techniques. Many of the tools and materials you use for this house will be useful for your future dream house. You may also decide you are really not interested in building dollhouses and can escape relatively unscathed financially while making some kid very happy. Probably, however, you will decide that building dollhouses is a very satisfying activity, as it gives you the opportunity to develop new skills and create a thing of beauty.

When you buy your kit, you may be able to substitute more expensive parts for less expensive ones, sort of like choosing more expensive carpeting instead of the standard carpeting in a tract home. You may decide you need windows that open and close, molding in every room, shutters, siding, shingles, doorknobs, plank flooring, etc. If these parts are all made by the same manufacturer, you may be able to get a better price by buying everything at once.

Be sure to have an overall plan of attack before you begin. Some manufacturers make special kits where the siding, trim, shingles, etc. have been premea-

An individualized dollhouse can look so authentic that you begin to imagine very small people living within, all with histories, romances, and adventures of their own.

sured and cut for your specific kit. There is definitely a preferred sequence of assembly and decorating and by buying everything at once, you can do things in the most expeditious way. You can also go broke.

ARCHITECTURAL STYLE

Determining the architectural style is one of the most important decisions you can make. It will dictate the style of everything else—wallpaper, shingles, molding and furniture. While there is no law that says you have to be consistent in your decor, you will probably be bitten by the consistency bug and want everything to be as authentic as possible. Since dollhouses are so small relative to a real house, you can see all the details at once, and differences in style or historical placement really stand out.

Basically, you'll choose between a city house or a farmhouse, with a lot of variation in between. City houses usually have mansard roofs and more formal doors and windows, such as French doors. They may have Palladian windows and formal architectural detail in the trim. Farmhouses range from the homestead-style house—a two-story box with a front porch—to a very elaborate Victorian farmhouse with gingerbread trim, wraparound porches, turrets and widow's walks. A separate subclassification is the Southern

If you've always yearned for a Victorian mansion but don't want to invest in a real one, a dollhouse is the perfect answer.

Display boxes are simple, inexpensive alternatives to a full-scale dollhouse. They can show off miniature furniture, dolls, or accessories. A removable glass partition protects your collectibles. Display boxes offer ample opportunities for specialty decorating—for example, a general store.

Traditional back-opening dollhouses show off the interior rooms to full advantage.

plantation house, which combines many of the features of the city house and the farmhouse. Most styles are available in every price range with the most elaborate ones in the high price range. Beyond the city house and the farmhouse, there are a number of speciality dollhouses, such as toolsheds and stores, as well as shadow boxes which serve

When closed, a front-opening dollhouse looks very attractive from the front.

as a frame for specialized miniature furniture and accessories.

LOCATION OF OPENINGS

Another big decision, one of the most important, is whether you want a dollhouse which opens at the back, at the front, or has multiple openings.

Back-opening dollhouses are the traditional type. The advantage of a back opening is that when you look into a dollhouse, you see the inside of doors and windows, which make rooms

look more authentic, and when you look at the front, you don't see any hinges. You can display only the front or the back of the house at any one time. However, a revolving platform is one answer to that problem (some even accommodate electrical wiring). You can finish the facing edges of the back walls with wood molding to hide the raw plywood. If you are afraid of dust or uninvited visitors to your carefully decorated rooms, you can buy hinged doors or plexiglass to

cover the back.

A front-opening house has a wonderful advantage: the front of the house is very attractive to look at when it is closed. When you open it, it feels like unwrapping a present. Most front-opening houses have a front which is divided into two or three sections and may also have a hinged roof over the attic. Each section is covered by a hinged door which serves as part of the exterior of the house. Front-opening houses are harder to work on during decoration as the hinged

sections are always swinging closed. If you take them off to make the work easier, the house looks unfinished. In any case, these sections get a lot of use, especially during assembly and decorating, and begin to show it.

Combination-opening houses have the advantages and disadvantages of both types. The most common kind has a section which is deeper than the rest of the house. This section has a

Combination-opening dollhouses offer the best of both worlds.

hinged wall at the front and the back is entirely open. This section is two rooms deep and may or may not be open for viewing through the two rooms. Some of the most elaborate houses even open on all four sides! You will probably choose the style you like and where it opens will seem secondary, but it is important to realize what the location of the opening will mean to you when you are working on it and when it is on display.

LOCATION

One of the most important questions to answer in making your decision about what kit to build is location—both the building site and the display site. The ideal building site is a workshop where sawdust, paint and glue are not going to be mortal enemies to the environment. You should realize before you begin that this is not a one- or two-weekend project.

The display site is also an important consideration. A finished dollhouse is a beautiful thing which can be displayed in any room. While most houses are very sturdy, there are certain

Combination-opening dollhouses are easy to work on.

With rooms added to each side, houses take on a new size and importance.

parts, such as porch railings and working windows, which cannot withstand a lot of rough use. Your display location should not be too accessible to people, especially little people, who are not going to treat your house with the proper respect. Kids seem to think that all dollhouses are toys (how foolish of them!) and are therefore fair game. You won't think it too fair when you find your porch railings on the floor.

You probably also don't realize how big a collector dollhouse is when finished. Even if you've chosen your dollhouse after seeing a model in a store, the completed house looks very large in a normal size room. Serious collectors have been known to build additions to their houses to accommodate their dollhouses. Some people, such as Flora Gill

Jacobs, the director of the Washington Dolls' House and Toys Museum, finally resort to opening a museum.

One way to decide on the best location is to find a cardboard

box approximately the size of your finished kit and put it on tables in various locations in your house. You may want to choose your exterior paint colors based on the room you will dis-

play the house in, so you should have a place in mind before you build. If you're not careful, you may be unable to get the completed dollhouse through a doorway and end up like the man who built a boat in his dining room and couldn't get it out of the house.

ABILITY

Your own level of competence is another factor in deciding which kit you choose. No skill required to build a dollhouse is beyond the capability of someone who can read this book, but some aspects can be utterly overwhelming to a novice, especially if you never did understand how electricity works or if you've never hammered a nail straight. You have to be a fairly exacting person to enjoy working on a dollhouse. (A dentist told me that he enjoyed working in small dark places so building a dollhouse was a perfect hobby for him.) Even if you are not a perfectionist or highly skilled, the challenge of following directions and doing something you didn't think you could do is very rewarding. One caveat: you must have the right tools. Probably the less experienced you are at building, the more important the right tools are.

TIME

The initial assembly time will probably take a beginner one to three eight-hour days. Exterior work, including shingling and siding, will take two days at least. Painting, because of the various coats required, can spread out over a week or two. Electrification of a medium to large house will probably take two days. Most interior decorating is relatively fast, but wooden plank floors, if they are laid one board at a time, take forever. Staining and varnishing interior woodwork also take a long time because of the many coats and sanding required and the time spent waiting for the pieces to dry.

Since hardly anyone has many full workdays to devote to a hobby, it is reasonable to expect that you will be building the house for at least three months, and it may take a year to complete. Where in your house can you leave a project set up for that time period where it will be safe from dust, the consumer testing of children and the other vagaries of everyday life, and still be a comfortable place to work? While it's possible to move the house after it is assembled, it's not something you will want to do after every building session. You may want to start in an unfinished workroom for the rough building and painting and then move the dollhouse—once—to a more comfortable area for all the finish work.

After you've spent hours gathering and studying information about various kits, gone to classes and read as much about dollhouses as you can, planned where and how and when you will build, it's time to go forth and buy your dollhouse kit.

Building dollhouses can escalate from hobby to obsession, as this collection suggests.

·2·

ASSEMBLY

No matter how exciting it is to buy a kit and bring it home, I've never met anyone who immediately started working on it. There's something terribly intimidating about a big, flat box that weighs about 50 pounds and is filled with lots of pieces of wood that in no way resemble a dollhouse. The pieces fit neatly in the box and the instruction booklet is about an inch thick. You know you've invested a lot of money, you may not be too sure of your own skills, and you really don't want to make a mistake. So, you carefully kick the box under the nearest table or bed and hope that it will build itself. Finally the thought of the money you've invested gets to you and, despite all your fears, you decide to begin.

Let me reassure you: building a dollhouse is not as difficult as it seems. You probably have already mastered a glue bottle and a hammer, and you can learn to con someone into helping you hold one wall while you glue on another. The most important thing you need is to know what your ultimate plan is. Do you want to electrify? Do you want to wallpaper? Will you put in plank flooring? If you have a clear picture of the finished product, you will be able to take steps in the basic assembly that will make life much easier.

THE FIRST STEP

The first step is to take all the pieces out of the box, unwrap them and look them over. Most instructions will give you a materials list; be sure that you have all the parts. However, the main purpose of checking the parts list against the actual parts is that you will never be able to get all the pieces back in the box neatly, so you will not be able to kick it back under the bed. What the heck—you might as well start.

LOCATION

We've already discussed location in the first chapter, but now that you are actually beginning, you will realize how important it is. Basic assembly will take about two days. You need a work space that will be undisturbed throughout this period, so if you use your kitchen be prepared to eat out.

Unless your worktable is truly a worktable and not a kitchen table, you should cover it with many layers of newspaper or flattened cardboard boxes and be sure the surface is level when you are done. As you move walls and floors around, you will gouge corners into the surface of the table, you will drop the hammer, you will drip glue, you will put heavy pieces on top of nail heads, which will sink into the table surface unless it is protected. At an arts supply store, you can buy a piece of vinyl used by graphic artists to cover their drawing boards. It heals itself when cut on and provides a nice smooth surface to work on.

The table should be at least one and a half times the size of the "footprint" of the finished house, so that you have a place to put your tools and the pieces you are working on as well as the pieces that are partially built. All dollhouse instructions tell you to work on a clean, uncluttered surface, but no surface will stay that way longer than 15 minutes. It's nice to have shelves nearby for the pieces that are drying or are in a holding pattern, so you don't knock them to the floor as you work on the next step.

The floor will suffer the same abuse as the table, so it should be easy to clean. Keep a broom, a small vacuum and a wet rag or sponge handy, so you can clean as you go. Sawdust has a habit of getting into glue and paint and should not be allowed in the same area. And there is nothing more frustrating than cleaning up dried paint while thinking about how easy it would have been to wipe it up when it was wet. Maybe these things won't

Some work can be done outside, where the mess won't matter.

happen when *you* are building a dollhouse, but it's better to feel superior when you are finished than to kick yourself for not taking steps to protect your person and your environment.

TOOLS

Tools make all the difference between what could have been an easy, neat job and one that is extremely difficult and not very successful. There are, of course, ideal tools, adequate tools and the ubiquitous kitchen knife. Ideal tools are expensive, and unless you already have them or want to go into dollhouse building professionally, you can probably do very well with a few basics. Of course, a few luxuries will make your life easier.

Basic Tools

Small hammer
Nails
Nail set or punch
Ruler, square and level
Small screwdriver
Razor knives
Small miter box
Trimming plane
Clamps, masking tape and
 rubber bands
Pencils
Wood fill
Wood or white glue
White paint
Paint brushes or small roller
Sandpaper and sanding tools
Rags, paper towels, cleaning
 materials
Optional: 15' roll of dollhouse
 electrical tape (if you intend
 to electrify the dollhouse)

Most of the required tools are notable primarily for their size.

A small miter box

First, you need a hammer—not a big, full-size hammer, but a small, seven-ounce hammer. (You will be using small nails in small places.) Many kits provide the required number of nails and a few extras—a reasonable amount for the experienced carpenter, so I suggest you take a sample to the hardware store and buy a few dozen more. This is a cheap investment considering the time you will spend on the floor looking for the last few nails which were swept off the table as the walls you were holding up came tumbling down. You also need a small nail set or punch to start holes with, a ruler, a square and a small level. These things have to fit into small places, so the old level you used to build your deck may not be appropriate. Get a pocket level. A small screwdriver or miniature screwdriver set (the kind with many interchangeable blades) is also required. There are not many screws in the typi-

cal dollhouse, but they are all very small.

Razor knives are necessities. They come in many varieties, but basically you need a pencil type with a swivel top which can accept a variety of sizes of blades or a utility knife. Be sure you have a supply of replacement blades, as a dull blade can do damage and make you crazy. A miniature miter box is very useful later for trim. You can buy a small one with a razor saw very inexpensively.

A trimming plane is a very small plane which allows you to trim off small protrusions and ragged edges on openings. Sometimes pieces just don't fit. This may be because you did something wrong, because the wood is warped or even because the kit makers made a mistake. You can sand edges forever to get them to fit or you can plane larger sections off easily. You have to be careful not to remove too much wood, but a trimming plane can make a tedious job easy and quick.

Clamps, rubber bands and masking tape will all hold pieces together while the glue dries. The clamps must be small and you will probably need a few. Joining some awkward pieces can only be managed by using thick rubber bands or masking tape to hold the pieces together during drying. Masking tape works very well for holding trim onto edges of walls or holding pieces together. You need a pencil—okay, you need more than one pencil, because one will always be on the floor or will have disappeared. Having extra rolls of masking tape and pencils available will save you hours of searching.

In addition to the tools, you also need a lot of cans and bottles of stuff—for example, a small can of wood putty or wood fill (the smaller the better; it will probably dry and harden before it is all used up) and wood glue—a lot of wood glue. Also called carpenter glue, wood glue looks like standard school glue but is yellow. It's cheaper in large bottles, so you should get one big bottle and a couple of the smallest bottles to refill as you use them. Some dollhouse assemblers suggest using white school glue, which is strong enough to hold any dollhouse together and dries transparently. It is also cheaper than wood glue.

Like pencils and rolls of masking tape, glue bottles tend to disappear under construction debris. Be sure you have more

Tools must be small for dollhouse construction.

Electrical tape

Small plane

Nail set

Razor knives

punch

Sanding tools

Level

Square

29

ings are invaluable, especially if they are labeled fully. If they aren't labelled enough, you should label them yourself. Be sure to keep these pictures available at all times or you will find that you have put a dormer on upside down or carefully attached a piece of molding to the wrong part of the roof.

Most instructions will include photographs of the house during assembly. Study these for clues as you go. I find the written instructions very important, but the pictures crucial.

Apply electrical tape. If you have decided you will electrify, you have purchased a 15' roll of

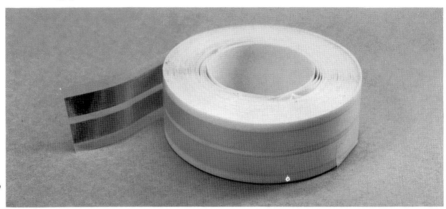

Right: Electrical tape comes in easy-to-use rolls. Below: The builder turned the house on its side in order to run electrical tape up the interior walls.

conductive tape from your dollhouse store. Find the sidewalls of the house and stick a piece of tape along the center of each sidewall (on the interior side). If the house is more than one room deep, make two vertical runs, one each at the center of each room. Leave about a 6" end at the lower edge and the top of the wall (or enough to reach the center of the ceiling of the attic). Keep the protective backing on these ends so that you can later stick them to the ceiling of the top floor of the corner rooms and use the lower end to attach the junction splice (the thing that connects the dollhouse wiring to the transformer). Leave the lower ends on all these vertical runs of wire so that you have the option of putting the junction splice wherever you want. By installing this vertical tape now, you always have the option of installing electricity without much trouble. If you wait until later, after you have wallpapered, you will have to drill through floors or make splices through floors. It is much easier to plan ahead.

Prepare for papering. Wallpapering can also be planned for at this time. On large sheets of kraft paper, trace all the walls you intend to wallpaper and identify the tracings carefully. Put them aside for later.

Align the pieces. Find the floor/ceiling pieces. Following the floor plans given in the instructions, mark the position of the second and third floors on the interior walls. Determine how the second and third floors will have to be assembled so that the stairway openings align properly. This may seem like a lot of work now, but will help you later get a square and level house, which is crucial for decorating and trimming.

Electrical tape in place up the side wall and in position to go over the roof.

glue than you think you need, because you do not want to run out in the middle of the job at 10 o'clock at night when all the stores are closed. Your options will be to call neighbors in search of emergency glue, which will further damage your reputation as a sensible member of the community, or to use your child's white glue.

Flat white paint is needed as a primer on ceilings; you may already have some around. Any paint will do as long as it is white so it won't show through the second coat. Good brushes are necessary if you don't want to pick hairs out of your paint. The exception is if you know you will be using a brush only once, and the paint or stain you are using is not water-based. After using the brush, throw it away dirty and avoid paint thinner.

A little edging roller is also useful for covering larger areas, and you'll need sandpaper, both medium and fine grain. Last, but not least, have a roll of paper towels, sponges, rags (I prefer old cloth diapers) and cleaning materials close at hand.

LUXURIES

I am often successful in putting off working on the dollhouse project of the month by deciding that I don't have the right tool to do the job. Each member of my family has at least five projects going at any one time, and it was incredibly hard to find tools I knew I already owned or to keep them from disappearing from my work area. Since dollhouse tools are very useful for lots of tasks, there is no solution to this problem except to wait for your

kids to grow up, to buy your mate his/her own set of tools and to vow that you will always put things away in their proper place. However, there is absolutely no guarantee that any of these will work. Keep in mind that some of the tools and materials used in dollhouse construction are dangerous if misused and should be kept out of harm's way, especially if there are children around.

We all have secret reasons for taking on a hobby, and it may be that you are a tool nut. (A tool nut is one who will bolt to the hardware store at the slightest suggestion.) If you are a tool nut, dollhouse building is a wonderful hobby. Let's take the basic list of assembly tools and see what is possible.

Hammer. Along with the basic wooden-handle-type hammers, which come in many different weights, you may also buy a metal hammer with interchangeable tips: round, flat and pointed, in plastic, brass or steel. A basic metal hammer with a small head is useful when installing electrical wiring. In the actual assembly of walls to floors, a bigger hammer is useful also, but you probably already have one of these.

Drill. The purpose of this tool is to make starter holes for nails or to make holes for electrical outlets. You can buy small hand or electric drills with an assortment of drill bits to make holes of various sizes, but in most cases you can pound in a nail to start a hole for a screw. Just be sure the nail is smaller than the screw.

Ruler, square and level. It's

hard to get too sophisticated with these tools except for looking for the smallest possible ruler and square. There are many kinds of levels, but you may want a short, ruler-type level as well as a small carpenter's square or plastic triangle which can be used up against walls. Squaring walls is an absolutely crucial part of construction; these these tools should be easy to use so you *will* use them and be very precise during assembly.

Screwdrivers. There are hundreds of varieties of screwdrivers available. A jeweler's set will be important later for more precise work, but the smallest cordless electric screwdriver with small interchangeable blades is very useful. You can't use it inside the dollhouse much, but many dollhouses have hinges and magnetic clasps which need to be screwed in to the outside. Electric screwdrivers save a lot of time.

Razor knives. You can buy specialized dollhouse kits which come in small wooden boxes with a variety of razor knives, blades, clamps, drill bits, sanders, etc. There is also an "art knife," which is a pencil-type knife with a flat extension on the middle. This makes it easier to hold and prevents it from falling off the table. You can also get small razor saws, which will be useful if you want to cut out extra windows or doors. There are miniature hand miter saws, which consist of a miter box and a razor saw holder that swivels to different angles; they are a little easier to use.

Miniature power tools. If you have the need, you can also buy miniature table saws, scroll saws, routers and combination tools. Other power tools look like electric screwdrivers but have many different tips, including sanding and buffing discs, screwdrivers and engravers. They have flexible extensions so you can reach into back corners and sand floors.

Clamps, masking tape and rubber bands. These are cheap and easy to use, but you may also want a small tabletop portable worktable. There are a number of brands on the market which have two halves that can move together and apart. You can hold wood between them to saw, you can clamp in a small miter box, you can cut on its surface with a razor knife.

Sandpaper and sanders. In addition to regular sandpaper, many small block sanders and sanding sticks for corners are available. These sticks are wrapped in sandpaper and work very well in small places. Small electric sanders can be used to sand larger expanses of wooden floors if you install the floors before you install the interior walls.

Wood putty, wood glue, white paint, brushes and small roller, rags, etc. It's almost impossible to spend more than is required on these items, but there are some especially good cleaning materials you should consider. You will need thinner or brush cleaner if you use oil-base paint or stain. There are also special cleaners available for removing latex paint, permanent marker, etc., from rugs, furniture and wood. It's a good idea to be prepared.

Paint. You don't have to buy the paint for the house before you begin assembly, but if you do you will have the option to paint trim, etc. before you put it on the house. I suggest you check your newspaper and see which store is having a paint sale. Go in and study the paint chip strips. You will probably want to paint the house in three colors: one for the siding, one for the roof and trim and a third color just to be tricky. A good combination is a dark roof, shutters and some trim, a medium color for the house and white or a light color for the window trim. In addition, you need white for ceilings. It may be cheaper to buy gallons of paint on sale than quarts not on sale.

If you do buy large containers of paint, take them home, mix them thoroughly and immediately put some in small plastic containers (pint or quart size). Then hide the big cans with the covers securely closed. You will probably find that there is a lot of activity around the dollhouse construction site. It is easy to knock over the paint or to kick over a can with a slightly loose lid as you are struggling with a recalcitrant nail or as you are furiously sanding a piece of siding. As a person who has mopped up a half gallon of light blue paint off a gray rug, I know whereof I speak.

These are just the many special tools available for the basic assembly. Wait until you get to flooring, molding, trim and furniture making! It's a tool nut's paradise.

STEPS IN ASSEMBLY

Now you have no more excuses.

You've got all the tools you need, the work area is ready and the time is now. Look over all the pieces and read through the instructions. Don't panic. If you do one step at a time, taking time to be sure you have the right pieces held in the right position, you'll be okay. You will probably find that building the shell is the easiest and most gratifying part of assembly. Unlike decorating the interior and exterior, there is an end to this step. Once it's built, it's built. You can add to it, but you never have to do it again, unless you build another dollhouse.

Label the pieces. Which brings us to a most important first step. With a pencil, label the outside of all exterior walls and the top of all floors and bases. Most pieces have one smoother side. If you are going to put siding on the house, put the rougher side to the outside. If you are going to put in flooring, use the smoother side for the ceilings. Some pieces have cutouts, and their position will determine which side is the outside. The rule is that the side of a piece which will be covered only by paint should be the smoothest initially. In any case, know which piece is which and where it belongs before you begin.

Label the drawings. Most kits will include many drawings of their houses from all different angles, including isometric views which show the position of moveable parts. You will have drawings from the back, front and sides, drawings that show assembled sections, drawings that show the house partially assembled and fully assembled. These draw-

Using the kit's floor plan and a pencil, mark the position of all the interior walls on the floors. By lightly drawing diagonals of opposite corners of each room, find the center of each room. If you are considering electrifying, drill a small hole in the center of each room. This gives you the option of carrying wire from one floor to the next through the ceilings.

Paint. With flat white paint, paint the ceilings of all the rooms. If you wait until the house is assembled, you will probably drip paint on the floor. You may also want to paint all the side and interior walls while you are at it. This first coat of paint is simply a primer. If you are going to wallpaper later, the paper will stick better to primed walls. Don't paint the floors.

Cut out windows and doors. You may want additional windows and doors in your house. One of the disadvantages of front-opening houses is that you don't see windows and doors when you look into the house so the rooms look very boxy. You may want to add doors and windows on the sidewalls to make your house more realistic. It is much easier to do this before assembly *if* you have measured very carefully. You've already marked the position of the walls and floors on the sidewalls and back pieces. Now, using the position of the existing door cutouts as a guide, mark the positions of the desired windows and doors. Cut out the openings. If you prefer, or you don't trust your measuring skills, you may cut them out after assembly, but it will be much harder. Remember that the back piece of plywood on a front-opening house is probably not as thick as the sidewalls so you will need windows and doors that adjust to walls of different thickness throughout the house.

Additional windows and doors can be added to the shell during assembly.

Square the openings. Even if you are not planning on putting in extra windows and doors, check the openings in your house. Often they will be cut out with rounded corners, but doors and windows have square corners. Now is the time to square the corners to make it easier to install the components later. Use a small saw and cut down into the corner, then cut horizontally into the corner. Hack around a little and the round corner will become square.

Check doors. If you are planning on putting in hardwood floors and interior doors, you should try fitting a door into the opening cut for it. Note how much space you have under the door. Will a piece of flooring fit under it or do you have to raise the door by cutting out the top of the door opening the same thickness as the flooring? If necessary, now is the time to do it. Use a razor knife, a small plane or razor saw. You'll be so proud of yourself later.

INSTRUCTIONS

Most dollhouse manufacturers are aware of how difficult it is to write clear instructions and are constantly trying to make them clearer to the beginner, but instructions are all written by experts who have built many dollhouses; what is perfectly clear to them may be very confusing to you. Every once in a while you will run across a sentence which makes absolutely no sense. That's because the instruction writer knew what he was talking about but hasn't told you. Don't assume you are stupid. Ask someone else if they can understand what is meant. If all else fails, call the manufacturer or the store where you bought the kit.

You will need both the written directions and the pictures to do a good job. If you can, pin the

If the precut openings for windows and doors are rounded when they come from the kit, they must be squared during assembly.

pictures up so you can constantly refer to them as you work. Check after each step that your house looks like the picture. This is not the time to get creative. There is probably a good reason for doing the assembly in the order given and for placing the walls exactly where they tell you to.

Always read the next step before you do anything permanent. For example, I very carefully constructed the basic box of a large rectangular shop, then measured and laid the floors, glued and nailed them. The next step was to attach hinges and the front-opening wall. It didn't fit. I had concentrated on the floor measurements and did not think about whether the front would fit. It should have fit, but it didn't. Because the glue had not dried, I was able to detach the front of the roof and move it up 1/4" and then everything was fine.

Don't quit for the day in the middle of a process and don't quit without reading the rest of the instructions for that part of assembly. Something that can be fixed 10 minutes after it is glued cannot be fixed 10 hours later.

During assembly, it's a good idea to have another person around. When you need an extra hand to hold a wall, another person is more convenient than a

Building and attaching the foundation, and weighting it down to dry.

vise. However, the main function of another person is to give you a second opinion. As the glue is drying, you may panic that you have done something wrong and need to fix it quick before the glue dries completely.

I recently put a house together perfectly—I thought—until I tried to fit a partial front to the shell. The door was on the wrong side! I moved the piece to the other side. Now the gable would be on the wrong side. I panicked. I ripped the house apart. I reassembled it inside out and then tried the front again. It was still wrong! People came running in response to my screams; one of them flipped the front over and it fit perfectly. It would

have fit the first time too. Sometimes we are so afraid we will do something wrong, we can't see that we've done it right.

ASSEMBLY STEPS

Not all houses are built in the same order, but there is a logical progression. For example, you must start at the bottom and work up. But, you may be told to assemble some components which require gluing before you begin actual assembly of the house so that they will be dry when you need to join them to the house shell later. Regardless of temptation, do whatever the instructions tell you in the order given (they probably know what they are talking about).

The foundation floor will probably be a piece of plywood with short sidewalls 1" to 2" high. Depending on the kit, the foundation may be fully built or partially built or completely unassembled. In any case, foundations are easily assembled. Usually you will build a base by arranging four side pieces in a square or rectangle, gluing their ends and then nailing them together. For large foundations, additional boards are nailed across the width to give added support. Usually attachments such as porches or extensions are built on their own foundations and added to the main house as one unit.

PORCHES AND OTHER TROUBLESOME PARTS

Most kits have porches because a nice porch is part of almost everyone's dream house. Porches add realism and romance to a house at the same time, but they are one of the hardest, most labor intensive parts of dollhouse building. The trouble with porches is that they have railings, and railings usually have to be built baluster by baluster. Many kits include little toothpick-like wood sticks which must be carefully spaced and glued into lower and upper railings. You have to keep them straight while they dry, you have to paint all sides of them, and for them to look good, you will probably want to paint the different parts different colors. You have to attach the railings to posts with glue because there is not enough wood to nail into. The railings are supposed to somehow stay glued to the posts without resting on the ground. Even the posts are usually only attached to the floor and the roof of the porch with glue. Porches have the most parts, are the most delicate, and are the hardest to paint of all the parts of the dollhouse. They are also the first thing a child will grab onto and the first thing to go on the exterior of the house. They are also part of almost every dollhouse.

So what's the solution? You must be very patient and very

Making the foundation for a porch.

careful as you work with the little pieces. It's probably best to make all the railings at one time when you are not tired or cranky or surrounded by tired and cranky people. If you paint the individual parts before you assemble them, you will find it remarkably easier to do a neat job. If you try to nail as well as glue wherever possible, the porch will be much more secure. Have lots of masking tape available to hold parts together, and measure, measure, measure, because the railings

must fit exactly between the posts. Too far apart, and they have nothing to hold onto; too close together, and they won't fit between the posts, which means your railing won't extend the length intended.

If you have the option, don't attach the porch until after you have finished siding or painting the exterior. It is a lot harder to work around a porch than to put the porch on a finished shell.

Don't put in the stairways, windows and doors until all the

exterior decorating is done and the flooring and wallpaper are finished. This will kill you because the house would look so much more finished if you could just add those parts, but don't do it now! As with a real house, the construction of the shell is quick, but the finishing takes forever.

THE SHELL
Nailing. Ultimately, dollhouses

Its foundation complete, the porch itself can get underway.

are held together by glue, but nails are used to hold the pieces together while the glue dries—a critical function. Most kits include different sizes of nails to go through the different thicknesses of plywood. You may have to countersink some nails when putting them through double thicknesses of 3/8" plywood. Countersinking means that you use the nail set to hammer the head of the nail into the wood. Be sure to use the right size nail. To make nailing easier, punch starter holes with your nail set or punch. You will then have a much better chance of nailing straight. If you don't nail straight, you can punch out the nails later and use wood fill.

Try to nail down on a horizontal surface, rather than into a vertical surface. Turn the house around or on its side or its roof or in whatever direction necessary to get the nailing surface under your hammer.

Most inexperienced carpenters tend to slant nails up or down. Pound all nails in far enough so you can check that the end will not pop out above or below where you wanted it to go, but leave enough head so you can pull it out if you missed. If you didn't miss, congratulations; pound in the head. (Just to make you feel better, let me tell you that I attended a seminar where the owners of two dollhouse companies assembled

A two-story porch adds special elegance to a traditional house.

dollhouses and both misnailed at least once.) Don't worry about making holes. If you put on siding, no one will ever see them. God made wood fill just so no one will know that you can't nail straight.

Gluing. Glue holds your house together, so you must use enough to completely cover a surface but not so much that you make a mess. Of course, you will have drips, but you can easily wipe them up if you do it right away. Don't apply glue until you have positioned all pieces dry to be sure they are in the right place. When you are sure you've got it right, measure again and try to keep the big picture in your mind. Glue the edges, then nail in place if necessary. You can use clamps to help hold the pieces together during nailing, but another human being comes in handy at this point because the pieces are big and awkward. Smaller pieces, such as landings, stairs or edge trim, can often be held together best with rubber bands or masking tape. Just let them dry completely before you remove whatever was holding them together.

Sidewalls. The most awkward part of assembly is putting up the sidewalls. You will probably have to nail the sidewalls into or along a groove in the foundation. Your sidewalls may have grooves at one side for insertion of the back or front. Be absolutely sure you know which is the front and which is the back of your house and that each piece is labelled appropriately. Start your nails in the sidewalls at foundation level. Do not go through the sidewall—just get the nails started. Remember, it is always easier to work horizontally than vertically, so try to work flat whenever you can.

A spacer helps to position the porch rails accurately.

Use the interior walls as measuring devices to determine the location of the floors, but do not install the interior walls until later. As a matter of fact, you may not want to install them until you have finished the interior flooring, because it is much easier to cover a big expanse with flooring than to cut pieces to fit each individual room. It is also easier to sand and stain floors without walls to bump into.

Holding a sidewall in place, place one of the interior walls against it, resting on the foundation. Draw a line on the sidewall, using the top of the interior wall as a guide; this marks the ceiling line of the first floor. Measure the thickness of the second floor and draw a parallel line that distance above the ceiling line of the first floor. This narrow band is where the second floor will join the sidewall. On the outside of the sidewall, start a row of nails in the center of these two lines for the second floor. Follow the same process for the second

On the outside of the sidewall, mark the position of the second floor.

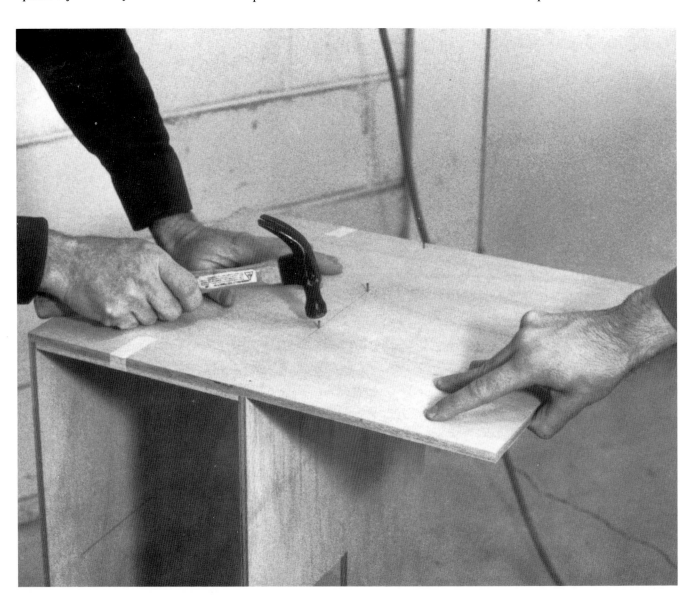

sidewall. Compare the placement of the second floor on the two walls. The measurements should be exactly the same. You may do the same for the third floor if it works for your kit.

Hold the first sidewall in position, checking for fit once again. Glue the contacting surfaces of the foundation and sidewall and then replace them together at a right angle. Drive the nails in. Do the same for the second sidewall.

Second floor. When placing the second floor, use the interior walls as measuring and supporting devices by placing them against the sidewalls and resting the second floor on top of them. Use your square to be sure all corners are right angles and use a little brute force to adjust them now, before you attach interior floors. The interior walls should be able to barely slide across the foundation floor, with the second floor resting evenly on top of them. Be sure you note the position of the stair

For easier building, turn the dollhouse so that you're nailing down.

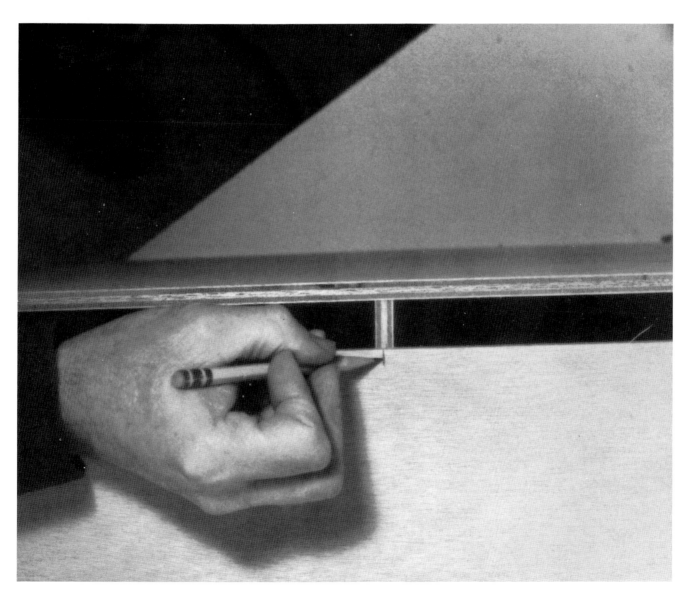

opening and compare it to the photographs; there is a front and back edge to the floors and if you ignore them, the stairway will not fit. Glue the contacting edges of floor and sidewalls and nail in place.

Position the third floor in the same manner, using the interior wall and noting again the position of the stair opening. In most kits it will come exactly above the lower opening, but the wall next to the stairs may be on the left or the right.

Stationary wall. The next step is to place the stationary wall, whether it's the back or front. With this wall held in position, draw lines above and below the set floors as markers for nail position. The top of this wall will probably be at the center of the attic floor. Depending on the

Add the stationary wall after the rest of the shell is put together.

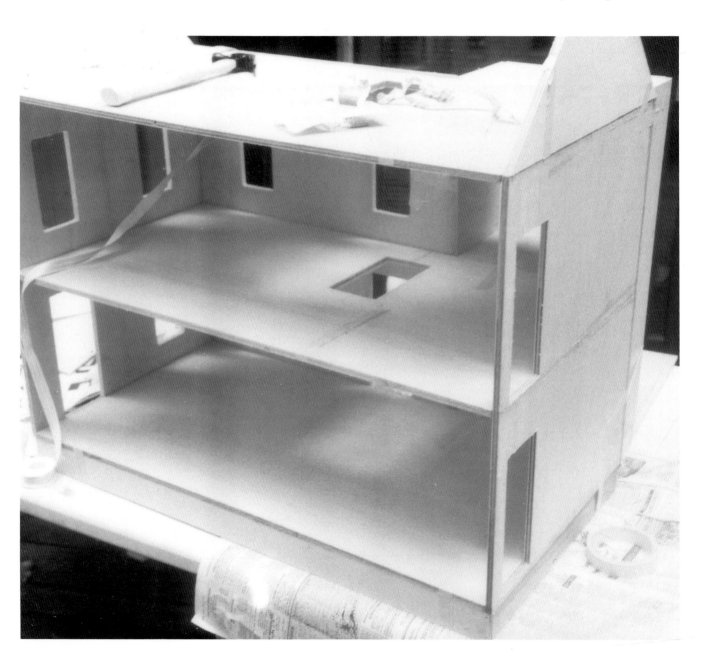

roof line and whether it is a back- or front-opening house, one long wall of the attic may be straight or both may be slanted with the pitch of the roof. Use your individual instructions as a guide for the placement of this wall. Make starter holes for the nails and glue contacting surfaces. This wall will make your house square. At this point you must check all wall and floor surfaces to be sure they are absolutely square and level. Make any necessary adjustments now, and pound in the nails.

ROOFS

Since there are many different roof styles, there is no one way to tell you how to assemble the roof in your kit. Your attic sidewalls may be part of the lower house or may be assembled separately. You may have a peaked or flat roof. You may have molding dividing the third floor from the lower house. Part of the roof may

Attic sidewalls support the roof.

be hinged, especially on a front-opening house. The assembly is basically the same on all houses, however. You must measure, nail and glue, checking that each piece is level, straight and true. If the pieces are not put in carefully, it will be very difficult to wallpaper, trim and put up molding.

Exterior trim may be part of the actual construction or may be pure decoration. You may want to consider painting some of the trim before you attach it permanently. You may also want to apply some kind of exterior finish, such as siding or brick, before you apply the trim. Check the pictures in your instructions and in the color advertising materials to see if this is a good idea. Remember: it is always easier to wait before you apply something than to permanently attach

Coordinating roof construction and siding can be tricky.

something and wish you hadn't.

These assembly instructions are meant as a supplement to the individual instructions in your kit. If you ever make a second house by a second manufacturer, you will be amazed at how different the suggested assembly details are. Each house is an individual and requires very specific instructions. Really complicated or custom houses may have master instructions and then separate instructions for components such as gables, roofs, dormers, porches, etc. These complicated houses are really a series of components

A carefully applied roof can be one of the most attractive features of a dollhouse.

and you do have some leeway as to the order in which you add the embellishments. After a few hours of construction, you will have three or four sets of instructions going and will have to relate one to another. The key is to put away parts (carefully labeled) and instructions (the appropriate set with the appropriate parts) when you are temporarily through with them.

MISTAKES

Now a word about mistakes. No matter how carefully you read the instructions, you will probably do something wrong. After all, a dollhouse is a fairly complicated structure with a lot of pieces. All of these pieces can be lost, put on backward, attached to the wrong part, or chewed by a goat. All of these things have happened to me.

In spite of all these mistakes, the houses I have built have come out beautifully because most of the mistakes were correctable or the broken piece was replaceable. Even if you do everything right during assembly, someone else will attempt to open the front of your house by pulling on a delicate porch railing, will forcibly open a window which was not meant to open, or will knock the whole house off a table. Most dollhouses will be touched and perhaps even played with and, like your real house, will require repairs. You might feel that you live with particularly destructive people when you find yourself repeatedly making repairs, but if you look at the way dollhouses are displayed in stores—on very high shelves or inside plastic boxes—you will realize that they are not meant to withstand rough treatment. So you will be making repairs unless you display the house where no one (including yourself) can touch it, and what fun is that? When something can not be repaired to look the way the original kitmaker intended, then creativity will, by necessity, turn a kit house into a truly individual creation. Even unfixable faults will be outshone by the total effect unless you point them out.

Don't point them out.

Roof, added porch, trim—all parts of the assembly should work together.

·3·

LIGHTS! ACTION!!

When I built my first collector dollhouse, it took me about six months to get it out of the box and two weeks of spare time to get it built, sided, shingled and painted. Then I stopped— because it was time to electrify. I kept moving the house from one location to another, thinking that if I put it where I would see it everyday, I would actually electrify.

One year passed. The guilt was building. I tried to get my husband, an electrical engineer, to help. He refused: his hands were too big, it was my project, I should learn how to do it, etc.

I was scared. Most women may be fully functioning human beings, but say "electricity" to them and they become toddlers with paper clips poised at an electrical outlet or mothers of toddlers with paper clips. Fear of electricity is a woman's birthright and her cultural heritage and is further exacerbated by the little red stickers on electrical appli-

ances which warn of high voltage. Men are not entirely immune from this fear either, though they may be better at hiding it. The biggest problem with electrification of dollhouses is fear—so let me dispel it.

ELECTRICITY 101

I was afraid I would hurt myself, the dollhouse or the entire electrical system of my house if I did anything wrong. I found out I couldn't because I was dealing with only a tiny amount of voltage.

The dangerous part of electricity is voltage. Let's compare the amounts used in a house, a dollhouse and a flashlight. The normal amount of voltage running through a household outlet is 110 volts in the United States (220 volts in Europe). Other countries have their own household voltage standards. A dollhouse electrical system runs on 12 volts. Now, a flashlight battery produces 1-1/2 volts. I don't know anyone

afraid of a flashlight. We use flashlights in the rain without fear of electrocution even if they have 10 batteries in them. The amount of electricity in a dollhouse is about the same as a large flashlight, so there is no reason to fear it either.

Electricity gets into a dollhouse through a transformer. A transformer plugs into the household current and transforms 110 (or 220) volts into 12 volts through the magic of science and two coils of wire. That's why it is called a transformer. Twelve volts will not hurt you. You would not feel the slightest shock if 12 volts ran through you instead of through the dollhouse. If you do something wrong in wiring the dollhouse, there might be a short circuit, which means you will hear a clicking sound and the lights in the dollhouse will go out. This will tell you that somewhere the electricity has hit a roadblock or that the two lines of electricity running through your house

A transformer converts household current into much lower voltage.

have met. Nothing you do in your dollhouse can hurt the electrical system in your house because of the transformer between the real house current and the dollhouse wiring. You are completely safe—honest.

The two strips of copper on the electrical tape used in most dollhouses work like two voltage pipes. One allows electricity to flow to an electrical appliance or bulb, and one sends it away. That's why all electrical circuits have two separate wires and why plugs have two prongs—one lets the electric current out of the source and the other returns it.

Think of electricity as a liquid that can travel in any direction as long as it flows along a conducting tape or wire. When a wire from a light sits in the middle of that liquid current, some of it flows up the wire, to the light, through the light, and down the other wire to the returning liquid current. If you have more

than one light on the same stretch of electrical tape, each draws enough current to make the lights work. The electrical path stops at the last light, goes across it and turns back.

If you have a lot of lights, you need a big transformer so there is enough current processed to feed all the lights. If you have only a few lights and a big transformer, it may feed too much current to the lights. It won't blow anything up, but it will shorten the life of your light bulbs. Light bulbs that consume too much current have shorter lives than the ones that consume only what they need. On the other hand, if you have too small a transformer and a lot of lights, the lights will be not as bright as they could be. Use the recommended size transformer and a regulator if necessary. A regulator regulates (what else?) the amount of electricity that flows from the transformer to the

bulb, preventing it from blowing out. All these recommendations will be given in the instructions for your wiring kit.

ELECTRICITY: WHO NEEDS IT?

You may wonder if electricity is really necessary. Of course it isn't, but neither are dollhouses. You've already spent a lot of money on this hobby, and you might as well light it up so people can see it and appreciate it. Besides, it's easier to work on the finishing details with the lights on. Just to test this theory, you may want to try a three-volt battery box, which is a battery holder with three plugs, disguised as a chest of furniture. It uses two C batteries and will light up to three miniature lights. Place one in a room, light it up and compare that room to the darkened one. You will want to electrify…or at least buy a few more battery holders.

A battery box disguised as a chest will light up a room.

KITS

There are a number of electrical wiring kits available, but basically you have to choose between tape kits and wire kits. Tape kits are easier to work with, and the tape is easier to hide under paint or wallpaper. If you are an electrician, you won't need a kit, but for the average bear, kits are ideal. Buying the components separately may be a problem if you don't know what you need, but the kit makers know what to include.

Kits are based on the number of bulbs which will operate in the dollhouse. You can buy a kit for one room (one to 10 bulbs), a small house (up to 16 bulbs) or a large house (up to 33 bulbs). They include enough tape or wire, the correct size transformer, lead-in wires, a junction splice, brads, a pilot hole punch, a test bulb or test probe, tiny brass brads and an instruction book.

The *conductive tape* or wire included in the kit is enough to install a reasonable number of outlets, but you may want to buy an additional roll so you can make electricity available in every room or on most walls. It is almost guaranteed that wherever you don't have tape on a wall, that is where you will want a lamp later.

A kit will include the correct size *transformer* for the number of bulbs suggested in the kit; you can easily upgrade to a larger transformer later, when you add more lights and appliances.

The *lead-in wire* has metal contacts that are screwed into the transformer, an on/off switch that will connect or disconnect the electricity flow into the house, and a small plug at the end. This end plugs into the junction splice, which is a small outlet that connects to the first tape run in the dollhouse.

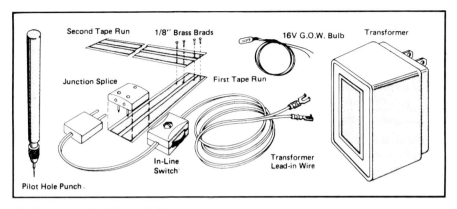

Equipment for electrifying a dollhouse

The *pilot hole punch* is a tool that makes starter holes for the brads to stick in. The *brass brads* are unbelievably tiny. There is no way that you will wire a house without losing a large percentage of them, because when you drop one it will instantly disappear. If you start out assuming that you need about twice as many as you and the kit maker think you need, you will save yourself a lot of frustration and considerable eyestrain.

The 16-volt *test bulb* or *test probe* allows you to see if the electricity is making it past any connection. Just poke the two prongs of the test probe into the conductive tape run with the electricity turned on. If that run is conducting electricity, the test probe will light up. The test probe is extremely easy to use and extremely useful during installation. After the house is completed, you can use it to find tape runs under the wallpaper.

TOOLS

You will also need a number of other common tools to install tape runs in your house, but you probably already have them from assembling of the dollhouse or in your junk drawer.

Razor knife
Scissors
Tweezers, needle-nose pliers
    or serrated-end forceps
Small hammer
Ruler
Screwdriver
Pencil

With a test bulb or test probe, you can check the current's flow.

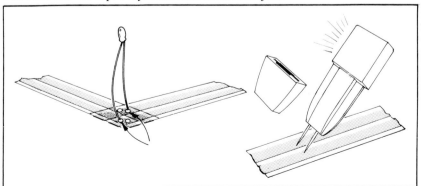

Of the above tools, some are made especially for miniature electrical work. You can get a small metal hammer to pound in the world's smallest brads, and small pliers or forceps to hold the brads. If you try to hold the brads with your fingers as you hammer them in, you will begin to seriously doubt your sanity. On the other hand, if you grab a brad with the tip of the forceps, stick the point of the brad in the foil, and push, the brad will stick in the wood. Then you can easily hammer it in. It's so much easier, you won't believe it. A jeweler's screwdriver with interchangeable blades is very useful for screwing in the junction splice, as well as for various other things.

THE PLAN AND THE TAPE

The first step in installation is to read through the instruction booklet and identify all the parts. The second step is to make a layout drawing or to copy a floor plan from the dollhouse instructions. Mark where you would like to place your lights and appliances. You have the option of ceiling lights, floor lamps, table lamps, wall sconces, chandeliers, kitchen ceiling fans, fireplace flickering lights, Christmas lights and more. You may also want coach lamps on the outside doors and porches.

When sketching out the layout, take into account what you want in the future as well as what you have today. You may want to use simple, inexpensive fixtures on the ceilings of all the rooms initially and supplement them with other lamps later. On your layout, mark the desired positions of your lighting fixtures and then figure out how to get electricity to them, using the shortest lengths of tape and making the fewest connections.

While tape can be placed on ceilings, walls or floors, in general I feel it's better to keep the

Electrification starts with a layout designed to fit your particular needs.

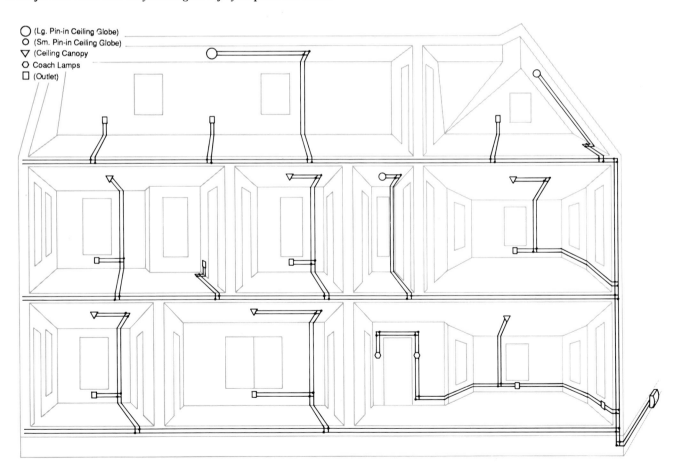

- ◯ (Lg. Pin-in Ceiling Globe)
- ○ (Sm. Pin-in Ceiling Globe)
- ▽ (Ceiling Canopy)
- ○ Coach Lamps
- ▢ (Outlet)

tape off the floors and use the walls and ceilings instead. You can run the tape around doorways and windows and the edges of walls to get it from room to room. You need to take into account any plans to lay permanent hardwood floors directly on the plywood of the house, whether you will have baseboard molding, etc. Flooring and molding will affect how high you need to place the tape on the walls in order for the lamp plugs to fit into outlets placed above the molding.

When you are satisfied with the layout, transfer the lines of your sketch to the actual house. With a pencil, mark the wall about 1" above the floor, which is where you will place the center of the tape. This 1" high placement allows for the normal height of any baseboard molding, plus the height of wall outlets. The top prong of a wall outlet must be able to fit into the top run of the tape. Very carefully measure this same distance from the floor in all the rooms so that you can count on this information later when you are searching for the tape under wallpaper. After the tape is installed, mark the position of the top and bottom copper foils on a business or index card. Later you can place this card against any wall in the house and find the tape.

THE JUNCTION SPLICE

Let's assume you took the easy way and did run the tape up the sidewalls during assembly. (If you didn't, there's no alternative but to read the kit's instruction manual to find an alternate

method.) Once you have drawn your proposed layout in all the rooms, the next step is to install the junction splice on one of the sidewall tapes. That tape will become your original tape run.

Installing the junction splice

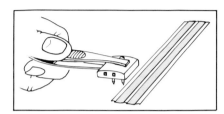

To install the junction splice, turn the house on one side. At the bottom of each sidewall, you should have a piece of tape with its protective backing still on. Remove the backing and attach the tape to the foundation in such a way that the junction splice will be under the house (if you prefer that it not show) or along the side of the foundation (for ease in plugging in the lead-in wire). You may think that aesthetically it is better to not have the junction splice showing, but it is far easier to make repairs or

check the system if the splice is located somewhere that can be easily reached without causing an earthquake every time you need to check the plug.

No matter where you install the junction splice, it is best to have the holes of the splice on the upper edge. When you plug in the lead-in wire, gravity will keep it in the junction splice. With tweezers, place the junction splice over the tape so that each point will be just slightly inserted into a separate copper foil. Put the junction splice aside and use the pilot hole punch to make starter holes at the tiny indentations you have just made in the copper. Take care not to make the holes too big because the points of the junction splice must be in contact with the copper. Reinsert the points of the junction splice,and gently tap in. Remember that the lead-in wire will be plugged into the junction splice, so make sure there is enough clearance to do that. Screw in the tiny screw on the junction splice.

Hold the transformer and loosen its two screws. Take the

The horseshoe-shaped connectors fit under the transformer's screws.

end of the lead-in wire that has two metal horseshoes, called "terminal connectors." Insert the terminal connectors under the transformer's screws, then tighten the screws. After you plug in the transformer to the house current and the lead-in wire to the junction splice, you will have electricity along the original tape run, which you can test with the test probe. If it doesn't light up, check all the connections to see if everything is tight and that the probe has one point in each piece of foil. The amazing thing is that it will work, and you will feel extremely successful.

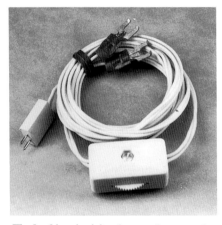

The lead-in wire joins the transformer and the junction splice.

Unplug the transformer and get to work. Take your roll of conductive tape and run it along your sketched lines. You can join additional runs of tape at any angle to earlier runs, although normally you will join runs at a right angle. To join two pieces of tape, simply overlap a new piece of tape over one which has been previously laid; then, using the punch tool, punch two holes diagonally in each piece of overlapping foil. Hold a brad with a pair of serrated nose pliers or forceps and stick its point in the starter hole, then pound in the brad.

Each intersection of tape will have four brads, two placed diagonally in each foil. The brads are placed diagonally to prevent short circuits. Because the brads are so little, there is actually plenty of room to place two brads in each overlapping foil. You can also fold the tape to form a right angle, but this is kind of lumpy and hard to cover.

The most daunting part of electrification may be keeping track of the tiny copper brads. One way is to stick a piece of double-faced masking tape on the table and place the brads on the tape. It is much easier to pick them up if they are not rolling around loosely. When you are finished for the day, you can roll up the tape, complete with brads.

Just remember that all the tape runs have to be connected directly or indirectly to the original run, which is connected to the transformer. The easiest way

to do this is to run one continuous tape, beginning at the original tape, around the inside of the exterior walls before you install the interior dividing walls. Then you will have electricity in all the rooms and you can easily add tape runs to interior walls if necessary. Otherwise, you can run tape through and around openings from one room to another on each floor. Then you can run short pieces up from this base tape to ceilings or walls. Since the electricity will always use the last electrical appliance to cross over and return, only one end of the tape has to be connected directly or indirectly to the transformer. Think of all of these pieces of tape as tributaries off the main river. As long as the runs of tape are connected to the main source of power, they will work.

If you really want to get sophisticated, add switches to individual rooms. To install a switch you must cut the flow of electricity on one of the tape runs and add another tape run

Two pieces of tape are usually joined at right angles.

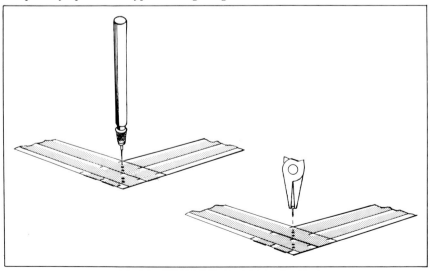

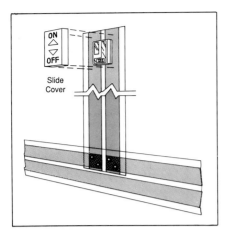

On-off switches can be installed for individual rooms.

to it. At the end of this new tape run, you install a switch which connects or disconnects the flow of current again. Wherever a switch is added, the current will be affected from that point forward. If you want only one room's current affected, you must place the switch on a short section of tape that isn't connected to any other rooms. The possibilities of switches are very interesting. You could arrange switches on upper floors and turn off all lights except the first floor, you can turn off ceiling lights while keeping desk lamps on, you could have a flickering fireplace in a darkened room. All it takes is a little planning.

If your house has any hinged walls, you can easily carry electricity to the hinged section. If there are two separate hinges, cut a piece of conductive tape down the center, producing two separate copper foils. Tape the foils between the hinge and the end of the tape run. Connect one foil to the top foil on the tape run, using brads in the usual way. At the hinge end, insert brads through the foil and

touching the hinge to make a copper-to-copper connection. Work the same way on the lower foil. If you prefer, or if the hinges are too far apart, use strands of wire (if you have directly wired some lights to the tape, you will probably have lengths of wire left from these lamps). Divide the wire into two separate wires at each end. Install the two wires to the tape run inside the house and to a tape run on the hinged wall. While this wire shows at the hinged edge of the door, it will be very unobtrusive.

Carrying electricity to a hinged section of the house

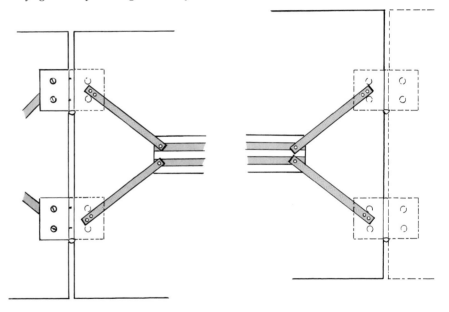

Remember that the tape can be hidden under wallpaper or paint and certainly will be hidden by any interior doors placed in the doorways. The tape is about the thickness of one coat of paint so if you prime your walls without painting the tape and then wallpaper or paint over it, you will probably not notice the tape. You can also sand the edges of the tape so there is a

smooth blending between it and the wall. The busier the print on wallpaper, the more concealing it will be. Don't expect the tape to totally disappear, however, as you will probably be able to find it by looking closely or by rubbing your finger along the wall. This isn't a big disadvantage as you may want to find it later.

CONNECTING THE LAMPS
While most lights come with a wire and a plug, you will find that you will be cutting off the plug and shortening the wire on all lamps which are wired directly to the copper foils. Ceiling and wall lamps are usually wired directly into the copper foils, although many miniature lamp manufacturers make canopy lights which have a base that plugs directly into the foil runs and the actual lamp or chandelier attaches or joins the base. Table and floor lamps can be plugged directly to wall outlets

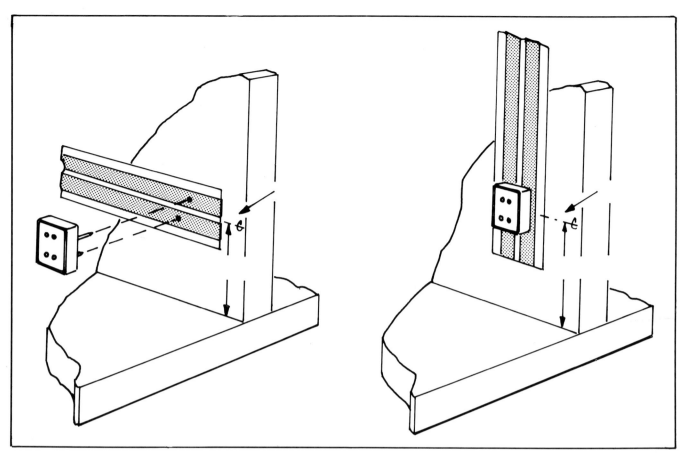

Wall outlets can be placed at the end of horizontal or vertical tape runs.

which are connected to the copper tape.

To wire directly to the copper foils, you must cut the wire coming off the lamp to the desired length. (I always cut mine about 1" longer than I think I need, so if I make a mistake, I can try again.) If you look closely at the wire coming out of a lamp, you'll see it has two sections. With a sharp razor knife, cut between the sections for about 1" from the end. Peel off the plastic covering of each section of wire. With a push pin, make a hole in each foil run. Insert one section of the wire into each hole and pound in a brad over it. Be sure the two sections of wire don't touch—the most common way of causing a short circuit.

You will find that there are two sizes of wall outlets: ones which are authentic and to scale in size and others which are larger but far easier to use. To install either kind of outlet, place the outlet over the foil just to make a small indentation. Then, with a push pin, make a hole in each indentation. Insert the wall plug into the holes. You can change the size of a larger plug to a smaller plug by cutting off the existing plug, exposing the wires and threading them in the holes of a replacement smaller plug. Do this if it is important to you to keep everything in scale in your house; otherwise, get both sizes of wall outlets and use them wherever appropriate.

The other option is to wire

all lights directly into the foil. It is very easy to remove brads and change the position of lamps by inserting a razor knife blade under the top of the brad and easing it out. Be sure the electricity is turned off when you do this.

TROUBLESHOOTING

In spite of your best efforts and extreme gratification every time you turn on the lights, there will come the day when you click the switch and nothing happens. It will be the same day that 10 people are looking over your shoulder to admire your work. If you secretly believe that electricity is magic, this won't surprise you. There has to be some rational explanation, however, and the chances are excellent that you will be able to locate the problem if you go about the search logically.

First, make sure the transformer is plugged into a live outlet. Sometimes house outlets are connected to switches and if the switch is not on, there is no electricity in the outlet. Our house is wired so that the top outlet in each plate is turned on by a switch and the lower one is always live. If you forget which outlets are live in your house, which I still do after 11 years, your problem may be solved after you replug into a live outlet.

After a few minutes, the transformer will feel slightly warm. Touch each point of the test probe to each screw on the transformer. You want metal-to-metal contact between each prong of the probe and each screw on the transformer, one-to-one. Take

care not to have one prong of the probe touch both screws. If you do, electricity will cross over the probe to the other screw, perhaps causing a spark. If the probe lights up, move to the plug end of the lead-in wire and touch one point of the probe to each point of the plug. The actual points do not have to touch, but the metal of each prong on the probe has to touch the metal of each prong on the plug. Again the probe should light up.

Now plug in the lead-in wire to the junction splice and test the prongs of the junction splice with your probe as above. (You will probably have to remove or at least loosen the junction splice from the wall to do this.) Again the probe should light up. Sometimes the position of the junction splice makes it very easy for the plug to fall out or get pulled out so you should make sure that a good connection is being

made. If the plug feels loose, slightly spread out the prongs on the plug to make it fit more securely or use a piece of tape to hold the plug and junction splice securely together. Once you are sure that these pieces are not likely to separate during use, you can assume that the problem is in the house wiring or in an individual light.

Light bulbs can be changed in a dollhouse by removing the brads which hold in the wires or by unplugging the lamp and reinstalling a fresh bulb. Light bulb extractors, which are long hollow tubes that fit over the tiny bulbs, are available to help with this task. Be sure the current is disconnected whenever you make a repair.

If you can't see an obvious problem, use your wiring layout as a guide and begin testing at the run of tape closest to the junction splice. Test the tape

To install a ceiling fixture, punch two holes, cut and strip the fixture's wires, insert wires into holes, and secure fixture.

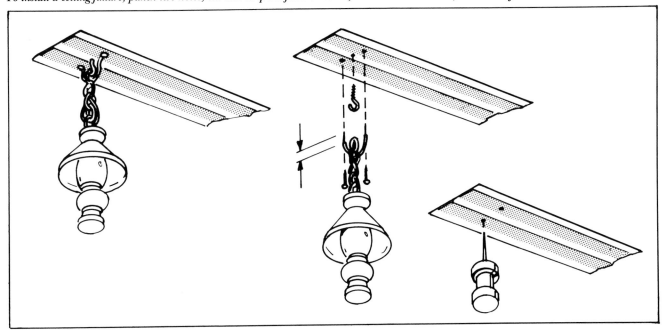

throughout the house with your probe until you find a spot where the probe doesn't light up. If you have been redecorating, you may have accidentally sliced the tape at some point. If you have removed and replaced any outlet or the junction splice repeatedly, the prong may have made the holes too big and you are no longer getting metal-to-metal contact. This can be remedied by splicing a fresh piece of tape over the damaged piece. Remember, if your electrical system worked once, it can be repaired. You just need to think logically and eliminate each possibility one at a time.

CHOOSING LAMPS

Ceiling lights with frosted or translucent glass shades are often seen throughout an older home and are one way to get light into every room of a dollhouse. These lights come in two styles: those that must be wired in and those that can be pinned in like a wall outlet. The pin-in type are usually called canopy lights and come in chandelier styles as well as modern globe styles. The choice of wire-in styles is even more extensive. Very elaborate wedding cake prism chandeliers, tulip shade hanging lamps, lamps with Tiffany, painted, rattan or green "case glass" shades are only part of the available selection.

Individual bulbs, either wired in or plugged in, can also be placed on the ceiling and covered with shades. Many ceiling lights are glued directly to the ceiling while others are suspended by chains with the wire woven

Table lamps add authenticity and warmth.

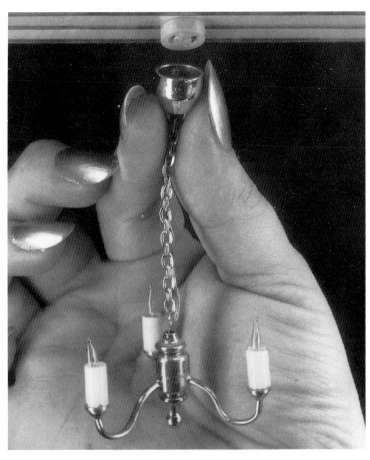

through it. In slanted attic ceilings, you may want to install inexpensive pin-in globes to the inside of the narrow rear roof so that they will light the attic without actually being seen. One especially interesting ceiling light is a fan-and-lamp combination which can be used in kitchens and bedrooms.

Wall lights are commonly used in dining rooms and hallways. Sconces are often made to match the shades used in chandeliers. Frosted tulip shades are especially attractive and are available in chandeliers, sconces, table and floor lamps.

Ceiling fixtures are available in styles to match any decorating scheme.

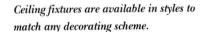

Other popular styles are candlesticks, gas lights and chimneys. Coach lamps are often used for exterior applications and track lights and picture lights are often used on walls.

Table lamps and floor lamps usually are available in matching sets. Most of these come with sticky bottoms because they are often top heavy and will fall over easily. Period lamps are often used in living rooms, bedrooms and libraries to add historical accuracy to a room.

There are also a number of other specialty lights available, such as flickering fireplace lights. These may be two light bulbs that alternately flash, bulbs embedded in logs to achieve a "glowing embers" look, or fireplaces which have been wired with flickering lights included. Outside post lanterns can be used in landscaping. Other specialty lights include Christmas lights for inside or outside the house and flashing lights for store windows. Even extension cords and electric meters are available.

While there are many other accessories, such as receptacles, outlet covers, toggle switches and fuse holders, a novice can easily electrify and fully light most single dollhouses, using the most basic equipment. After you've electrified once, you will feel so satisfied with yourself you may want to go out and buy another house just to show off your skill. Or at least you will be able to say, "Of course I electrified the house. Nothing to it."

Regardless of the period you've created in your dollhouse, there are lamps to match.

·4·

INTERIOR DECORATING

Congratulations! The shell is built. Now you have to decide what to do next. There really is no set order of which interior and exterior projects must be done when, but any job which requires moving or turning the entire house should be completed before any delicate work is done. A messy job involving lots of painting, sanding or gluing should be done before such finish work as wallpapering or installing delicate light fixtures. So, although the next two chapters divide the work by interior and exterior projects, you will probably work on the big, messy jobs first, whether they are on the inside or outside. Read the next two chapters, decide which projects are appropriate to your house, make a list, put the projects in a logical order and then begin.

A dollhouse is a frame on a miniature portrait of rooms, each of which is a moment in time. When you look inside a dollhouse, you see the entire life of a family frozen in a time warp. You also see fine craftsmanship and careful attention to detail. Dollhouses are so fascinating that museums all over the world display them and people return to see them year after year. The Colleen Moore dollhouse exhibited at the Chicago Museum of Science and Industry was my first inspiration, although I was amazed at how much smaller it got as I got bigger. Other magnificent and historical dollhouses are displayed at the Legoland Museum in Denmark and the Washington Dolls' House and Toy Museum in Washington, D.C.

While few dollhouses ever reach that level of perfection and luxury, there are still many options in decorating, which can be divided into two philosophies: the theory of evolution and the theory of creation.

THE THEORY OF EVOLUTION
Many would-be miniaturists get involved in the hobby first because they fall in love with some accessory or tiny piece of furniture they see in a toy or antique store. One piece leads to another and soon they need to buy a dollhouse to give their collection a home. If they have been particular in their love affair, they will have collected a homogeneous assortment of furniture and accessories and will build a dollhouse to suit it. If they have been whimsical in their approach, they will have a hodgepodge of goodies to fill a house.

THE THEORY OF CREATION
The other approach to dollhouse decoration is to create an image in your mind of the finished house and to build, buy and beautify with that image in mind. You might start with one beautiful piece of furniture and build a dollhouse to fit it, or you might start with a house built in a certain architectural style and decorate and collect with that style in mind.

AUTHENTICITY VERSUS ECCENTRICITY

While it is a good goal to be historically accurate in decorating your dollhouse, no one has decreed that your dollhouse has to be 100 percent located in any time period or that all your furniture must match or that there be no anachronisms in any of the rooms. Most of our own houses are eclectic mixtures of good pieces of furniture and beat-up old favorite chairs. There are many modern houses today which are furnished in antiques and are lived in by thoroughly modern people who leave their thoroughly modern belongings all over. Many of our houses have very modern kitchens and very countrified living rooms. The difference with a dollhouse, however, is that you see all of the rooms at once. There should be some consistency in either color or style, or some recurring element in all the rooms to tie them together.

FURNITURE

Dollhouse furnishings tend to fall into four historical periods: the late 1890s, the Depression era, the 1940s, and the contemporary period. This is by no means the complete range of historical periods. Every style of the furniture is available, from Colonial to Victorian.

The wood is either painted or made to look like oak, walnut or mahogany. As a very general rule, oak is usually used in the older farm houses, mahogany is used for formal rooms and formal houses, painted furniture is used primarily in modern houses and walnut is used in all types.

Often the time period represented in the dollhouse is most obvious in the kitchens and the bathrooms. The oldest houses will have pump sinks, wood stoves and wooden iceboxes. The 1920s houses will have

A kitchen in a Tudor-style house

porcelain sinks, four-burner gas stoves and more sophisticated iceboxes. The 1940s house will have a standard kitchen sink, a refrigerator with compressor on top and a gas stove. The modern kitchen will usually have modern appliances coordinated with painted cabinets.

Storage cupboards also reveal their history—from Hoosier cupboards with built-in flour bins, marble top cupboards, bakery racks, metal cabinets or sleek built-in cabinets of the modern period. The time placement will be unmistakable in a well-designed kitchen. In our own kitchens, we may use country furniture

and sleek European appliances in one space and our dollhouse kitchens may be somewhat eclectic too, but one should avoid obvious modern touches in a kitchen which is in every other way dated before those things were invented or designed.

Bathrooms change with each historical time period as well. The oldest houses will not have indoor plumbing, but will have a privy outside. Slightly more modern houses will have wall-hung tank toilets and claw foot tubs. Bathroom fixtures are available in a variety of styles; some are decorated and painted, and some look like the most modern

of fixtures.

Each of the bedrooms can show the style and the needs of its occupants as well as the historical placement of the house. Most houses will have a formal master bedroom. Beds are available in every style, from Queen Anne to Victorian to Colonial. Canopied beds are especially charming. The linens on the beds and the drapes on the wall further carry out the selected mood and time.

It seems that most dollhouses have a nursery, probably because

A German turn-of-the-century kitchen

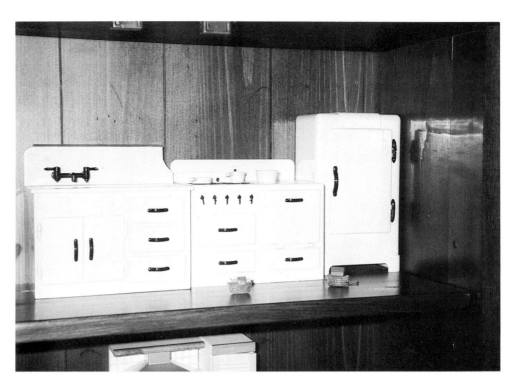

Kitchen furniture can range from stark 1940s style to cozy Early American.

it is so much fun to decorate. Often, there will be a carriage, a cradle and a crib. There is a wide assortment of furniture and accessories for the baby's room, from romantic Victorian cribs to modern changing tables.

Children's rooms can also be decorated to suit any historical period. Your doll child can have a sleigh bed or a bunk bed with matching dressers, night stands and desks. The nicest thing about children's bedrooms in a dollhouse is that they stay neat

Bathroom appliances can fit any period or decor.

which, of course, can make them look a little less than authentic.

The remaining rooms in your dollhouse are a real test of your own creativity and individuality. Typical dollhouses will have a playroom, attic, library or study, sewing room, grandma's room or music room to fill the space not occupied by the family's main living quarters. Specialty dollhouses are built as stores, workshops, stables or barns and can be decorated appropriately by furniture specially made for these uses: display cabinets, magazine racks, rocking horses, toy chests, worktables, stalls, etc.

FURNITURE KITS

Furniture can be bought assembled and finished, but there are also kits available in every possible style. After a while, you may not be satisfied with the furniture which is ready-made. While it looks good superficially and is often true to a historical period, it is mass-produced and will not stand up to heavy use. Often the brass pulls will fall off or the delicate legs will break. These things can all be repaired with glue, but there may come a time when you want to make your own furniture from a kit or from scratch.

Often pieces which are too expensive to be mass-produced because of the labor required are available only in kits. For example, you can make rope beds, porch swings, rolltop desks, even mattresses from a kit. In some cases, kit furniture may be less expensive than ready-made, but not always. The quality of the components may be better in these kits and may have been made individually. If you are considering making your own furniture, it is a good idea to make a few kits first so that you will understand the delicacy

of the work and the tools required. One particularly useful tool is a magnifying glass on a stand which has multiple clamps, vises and grabbers to hold pieces while you are working on them.

BUILDING FROM SCRATCH

If you're a person interested in a challenge, you can create original pieces or reproduce a beloved piece of full-size furniture. A well-stocked dollhouse store will provide everything necessary.

The standard parts of furniture are available as separate components: brass pulls, spindles, legs and posts. Standard size strip and hobby wood is available in plywood, basswood and balsa wood.

Some types of furniture which may not appeal to the general public, such as furniture from the 50s, may be available only if you make it yourself. Some companies offer kitchen cabinet fronts and bases so you can build in cabinets just as you would in a modern kitchen. You can get everything you need—even the kitchen sink.

A wonderful source of inspiration for new projects are miniaturist magazines such as *Nutshell News* which publish projects every month for furniture and accessories and also illustrate some beautiful dollhouses fully decorated in a multitude of styles. Some of the articles give general ideas you can adapt to your own dollhouse, while others give specific projects, com-

Even for a screened porch, accessories can be bought or built.

ACCESSORIES: USEFUL MATERIALS AND FOUND OBJECTS

• • •

Modeling material to make food, plates, decorative edges, etc.

Floral tape and ribbon to make flowers and plants.

Small plastic foam balls to use as molds for round objects such as pumpkins, heads, etc.

Foam cups, cut in ovals and painted to make garden stones.

Hairspray to set pleats and draping of fabric.

Sandpaper to make shingles or tarpaper to cover flat roofs, or to cover any rough surface, including textured walls and ceilings.

Greeting cards and manila folders for book covers, boxes, suitcases and baskets.

Plastic and paper tubes from fax or other office paper, cut into cakes, pillars, pedestals, etc.

Foam board cut to size and covered with wallpaper or flooring to make removable walls and floors.

plete with step-by-step instructions. They range from the simplest ideas (how to make a toilet brush using a pipe cleaner and balsa wood handle) to a complete 1950s bedroom. It is definitely worth having a subscription to keep your creative juices flowing.

While you gradually build your collection of furniture, you can make do with found objects and other people's rejects. Remember that you can make simple furniture from common household items such as thimbles, thread spools, bottle caps and shishkebob skewers.

■ You can paint or cover small cardboard boxes with wallpaper to make dressers, beds, fireplaces.

■ Fit a box lid with shelves to make bookshelves.

■ Small plastic caps and lids can be converted into tables or stools by covering them with tablecloths.

■ Mirrors can be cut out of foil pie pans and framed with clay

ornamentation.

■ The little plastic doodad that keeps the cheese off a pizza box becomes a table.

■ Children often enjoy recycling their found treasures into dollhouse furniture. Just remember to keep the 1" to 1' scale in mind.

These pieces can be discarded as you replace them with "real" furniture as your collection grows or you may hold onto them with fond remembrances of when your dollhouse was new.

ACCESSORIES

Accessories account more for the "Ah" factor than any other aspect of the dollhouse. "Ah, look at that!" onlookers say, when they see a tiny piggy bank in a child's room or a basket of corn on the cob with "real" cornsilk. The "Ah" factor is what normal miniaturists are striving for.

A tiny philodendron, a pair of miniature candlesticks, an oil-burning lamp— accessories add charm to a dollhouse.

Museum dollhouses, on the other hand, are filled with the "Wow" factor. Some of the more fabulous dollhouses seen in museums have miniature Bibles with the actual New Testament printed in microscopic print, fully operational musical instruments, diamond-studded tiaras and other spectacular items. You can't look at them without saying, "Wow, that's fantastic!" The house you decorate will probably not be filled with wows, but it can produce plenty of ahs. Just like a real house, a dollhouse is just a shell until the everyday accoutrements of daily life fill the rooms.

Every room needs to have an identity. Often the more specific its use, the easier it is to decorate in an interesting way. Because the kitchen has a specific purpose and its furnishings are distinctly tied to a historical period, it is easy to fill with items which emphasize that time period. The labor-saving devices found in a kitchen will vary from a butter churn to a toaster, depending on historical placement. The china and cooking utensils also tell the observer a lot about the date of the house.

Even food comes packaged differently depending on the time period: eggs in a wire basket or eggs in an egg carton. Practically every kind of food is available in miniature form, from plates of cold-cuts and varieties of fresh vegetables to glasses of milk, souffles and pizza. Just as in real life, miniature food can be very tempting. It's hard to pass up a display of food in a store without wanting to stock your own cupboards.

Often small vignettes, or little scenes, can be created by placing objects on the tables so that a room looks as if the people who live there have just stepped out. These objects can be purchased individually and worked into

Whatever their period, kitchens can have the appropriate tools and containers.

Dowels of varying lengths and diameters for curtain rods, table and chair legs, and handles for brushes, brooms and garden tools.

Pipe cleaners for brushes and brooms.

Necklace chains for hanging lights and Christmas tree garlands; watch faces for clocks; earrings and pins as plaques; jewelry to decorate frames and other "objets d'art."

Rickrack and lace for curtains.

Microscope slides for stained glass inserts and glass shelves.

Molded plastic blister packages for windows and glass panes.

Fringe or whisk broom bristles for thatched roofs and haystacks.

Fringe to make broom bristles.

Nylons for window screens.

Popsicle sticks for picnic tables and siding on outbuildings.

Mail order catalogues, book club ads and record club ads for book jackets, record covers and artwork.

Restaurant butter or jelly single-serving containers for sinks or wash pans.

Hospital pill paper cups for lampshades.

Embroidery floss and straight pins for knitting and crochet projects.

Thread and film spools for lamps and tables.

The plastic device that keeps pizza from touching the top of the box for a table.

Wooden coffee stirrers to make shovels and scoops.

Thimbles—metal for buckets, porcelain for lamp shades.

Children's game pieces, plastic people, Crackerjack prizes, miniature pencil sharpeners and erasers for ready-made miniatures.

Sequins, snaps or buttons as wheels or smoke detectors; dress hooks as cup hooks.

Twigs as firewood; pebbles for garden walls; sifted garden dirt for landscaping.

Tiny mirrors and framed pictures are easy to construct.

your own vignettes or you can buy vignettes already prepared, such as a half-carved pumpkin with its insides beside it on a newspaper, or Easter eggs in the process of being colored.

In the dining room, you will probably want more formal dishes and linens. A "silver" tea set looks attractive on the sideboard and you may want a punch bowl and cups for entertaining. Every dining room needs candlesticks and candles and you may also want "pewter" goblets for a formal room. You can decorate the dining room for the season. A plate of Easter eggs or a turkey on a platter can set a holiday tone for the whole house. Seasonal decoration can also be used in the living room. Christmas trees or Easter baskets by the door can set a holiday mood. Even the upholstery or

drapes can be changed to suggest winter or summer.

Bookcases are available in unfinished wood and can be stained or painted to match your decor; you can purchase them finished as well. Many sizes, including corner bookcases, are available and they are one of the easiest types of furniture to build in. Bookcases are especially useful in making a room look real, filled with books and small curios to capture the feeling of a family and a time. They can also be used in kitchens or dining rooms and are especially useful in decorating stores.

■ As a reminder of your own early decorating days, you may want to make a bookcase out of bricks and strips of 1"-wide wood.

Mirrors can be a very effective decoration of many rooms of a dollhouse. Not only can the frames reflect the historical period, such as "gilded" ornate frames in a formal Victorian room, they can also reflect the decorations on opposite walls and make a room seem larger. Often curio cabinets, hall stands, bedroom dressers and armoires include mirrors. Consider using mirrors in hallways to add interest and the illusion of space to these functional areas.

Paintings and portraits also add to the realism of the interior. Many companies reduce actual etchings, advertising posters and old photographs to 1/12 scale. They may be already framed or frames may be purchased separately.

■ Old family photographs could be reprinted and individual heads can be cut out and framed.

■ Small mirrors can also be glued to a wooden backing and decorated with modeling clay or framed like a photograph.

■ Good sources for art prints are museum catalogues. They may show tiny versions of the available prints and these advertisements are the perfect size for a dollhouse.

■ You may consider choosing some postage stamps which are reproductions of etched portraits of Johns Hopkins, Susan Anthony, Dorothea Dix or Margaret Mitchell and framing them yourself.

■ Using a miniature miter box and razor saw, you can easily make your own frames from thin wood strips available at hobby shops and a thin base of plywood or balsa. Glue the stamp or picture to the base, then cut out strips of wood and miter the corners to fit and glue in place. If you paint or stain the wood

Even daily chores seem charming when they're cut down to size.

first, the frame will be complete when it dries. If you want to make the picture larger than the stamp, use a soft pencil and sketch an oval around the portrait, using a dotted line. Then shade in the area between the oval and the frame.

Upstairs, the bathroom is one of the most interesting rooms to decorate. Linoleum or tile can be laid on the floor and the walls. Vanities can be strewn with bottles and toiletries and other accessories, such as toilet paper rolls, add authenticity to the room.

■ Towel racks and shower curtain rods can be made of small wooden dowels glued to small circles of 1/4" balsa wood. Poke a hole in the center of these circles halfway through the thickness of the wood and insert the dowel; then glue the circles to the wall.

If you have chosen to make an extra room in your dollhouse to reflect one of your own personal interests, you will find plenty of accessories available for practically any hobby. For sewing rooms, you will find a wide assortment of sewing machines, dressmaker's dummies, bolts of fabric, scissors, cutting boards and ironing boards.

■ Fabric swatches and yarn balls can be made from your own supplies. Be sure to choose small prints and fine yarn to keep the proportions right.

Other rooms have their own delights. Playrooms can be filled with hundreds of kinds of miniature toys, including miniature dollhouses. Libraries, studies and dens can be furnished with rolltop desks, globes, desk lamps and large selections of books. Most musical instruments have miniature versions to enliven a music room. You may have a laundry room or pantry which you can fill with brooms and cleaning supplies. Sometimes the most mundane objects in a real house are the ones which inspire the greatest number of "Ahs" in a dollhouse. Things like a wrapped parcel with stamps or a detergent box cause the most excitement because they make the house seem like a home.

FIREPLACES

There is nothing like the combination of a fireplace with flickering flames showing through logs on a grate with a brass firescreen to warm up a living room. Fireplace tools and a clock on the mantle add to the effect. Some fireplaces are prewired for flickering flames, but most can be adapted for electricity by drilling a hole in the back to pull the wires through.

There are many fireplace kits available, as well as unfinished fireplaces which can be painted or stained. Fireplaces come in many styles, from simple rectangles to those with elaborately carved mantle pieces, and you should choose the finish based on the furniture style.

■ You can make a marble fireplace by using a marbelization kit available in craft stores. Since these kits are meant to be used on full-size furniture, you will have to adapt the instructions to miniature by using smaller brushes to make tiny streaks and grain.

If you plan on making a brick fireplace, choose a kit fireplace with very simple lines or make one yourself.

■ You can provide your own logs by picking up tiny twigs outside.

BRICK FIREPLACE

From 1/4" thick plywood or balsa wood, cut out a base 6" x 1-1/2" wide. From balsa blocks, cut out two posts 3/4" thick and 3" long by 1-1/4" wide, and a mantle 1-1/2" wide, 1-1/2" thick and 5-1/2" long. Cut out a piece of 1/4" plywood 1-1/2" wide and 6" long. Cut out a piece of 1/4" plywood or balsa wood 4-1/2" tall and 5" wide for the backing. Paint the top with white enamel. Paint the backing black. Purchase approximately 50 miniature bricks 3/4" long, tile mastic and grout.

Glue the mantle across the top of the backing with 1/4" overhanging. Glue the posts under the mantle at each edge. Let dry. Apply tile mastic across the top of one of the posts a few inches at a time. Lay the bricks on the post, one by one, staggering the bricks. On the first row, lay two bricks with the edges of the brick overlapping the sides of the post by 1/8". Stagger the second row by beginning and ending with a half brick. (Bricks can be broken with tile snips or two pairs of pliers. Mark the center of the brick. Hold the brick with one pliers at the halfway mark, grab the second half with the second pliers, and bend.)

Continue up the post. Adjust the distance between the bricks so they come out evenly at the top of the posts (10 runs of brick). Work one row of bricks along the lower edge of the mantle, then work down the second post. Complete the mantle (5 runs of brick). Work the second post in the same way. Brick along the sides of the post

and the mantle piece and under the top edge. Center the fireplace on the base, with back edges even, and glue in place. Brick the base and edges of brick. Center the top on the mantle with back edges even and glue in place.

WALLS AND CEILINGS

One way to get a sense of consistency is with wallpaper and paint. Choose one color and use it throughout all the rooms. For example, you may choose blue as your base color and then use various shades of blue throughout the house. Your living room might be slate blue while your nursery is baby blue. The kitchen wallpaper may have small blue flowers on a white background, but there should be some blue in all of the rooms. Then when you look at the house, there will be the same blue current running through all of them. To further enhance that feeling of unity, paint the facing edges of the interior and exterior walls and floors in that color before you wallpaper or wallpaper over the facing edges of walls.

Choosing wallpaper. The same guidelines which apply to choosing wallpaper in your home apply to dollhouse wallpaper. Because you must keep the 1" to 1' scale in mind to avoid overpowering delicate furniture and accessories, you will probably choose dollhouse wallpaper over "real" wallpaper.

Wallpaper definitely makes a statement about historical placement, and it is possible to find historically accurate wallpaper for any period. Remember that the smaller and busier the print, the more flaws and electrical tape it will cover and the easier it will be to match. On the other hand, larger prints with light backgrounds will lighten up dark rooms.

Many wallpaper designs come with coordinating prints and solids as well as matching borders so you can easily find a way to wallpaper any room. You may want to wallpaper only part of a wall. If you install a chair rail in a house, you may want to wallpaper above the chair rail and paint in a complementary color below. Kitchens and bathrooms often look good with just a border along the ceiling or above the tile walls.

Applying wallpaper. This is easier than in a real house. Prime all walls to be wallpapered with latex or acrylic paint, and then sand them. Cut the wallpaper 1/8" less than the height of the wall, because wallpaper will stretch when applied. Most rooms will require three to four sheets of wallpaper. Cut as many pieces of wallpaper as needed, matching the design where sheets will join. If you have traced the walls on paper as suggested in the assembly chapter, you can use these tracings to measure. Buy premixed wallpaper adhesive, the same kind you use on regular wallpaper. Apply the adhesive on the wrong side of the paper. Begin at an outside edge of one wall and apply the paper, smoothing out bubbles as you go. Cover right over windows and doors and crease at corners to fold. When the wallpaper dries, use a razor knife to cut out openings.

Leftover wallpaper can be used to decorate found objects and turn them into furniture.
■ Small cardboard boxes can become tables or bases for beds.
■ Headboards for beds can be made from small pieces of cardboard cut to fit and covered in wallpaper to match the walls of a room.
■ Cornices above windows can be made from sections of cardboard boxes and covered in matching wallpaper.

Walls may also be painted in flat latex paint. Plan on at least two coats of paint, sanding before each coat. Dollhouse walls are made of raw wood, as opposed to the drywall or plaster of real houses, and need considerable work and paint to look as smooth as a wall in a full-scale house.

One way to decorate plain painted walls is with a wallpaper border, running along the top of the walls or 3" above the floor as a pseudo chair rail. You may want to stencil a design instead of using a wallpaper border. Miniature stencils can be purchased or designed yourself. Use the same materials as those used for regular stencils, but make your designs in proportion to dollhouse size.

Walls can also be paneled in wainscoting, sheets of thin wood scribed to look like narrow strips.

Left: Miniature wallpaper.
Right: Modeling material and tools.

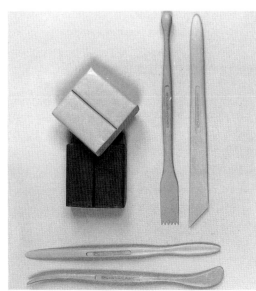

These are placed vertically on the lower half of walls with a thin piece of molding like chair rail on top. For more formal rooms, raised panels of wood can cover the walls and be stained to match other woodwork in the room. Molded wainscot panels, fireplace mantles and elaborate trim are also available in plaster for the most formal of rooms. Fancy trim and decorations can also be made from modeling material.

Ceilings can be painted, but they can also be covered in tin panels to duplicate the look of turn-of-the-century ceilings. For formal rooms, plaster ceiling appliques come in every possible style and can be applied singly or in groups. Complete ceilings with center and edge designs are available in sheets of different sizes and can be trimmed with plaster moldings on the side walls. Ceiling appliques can also be made of modeling material, papier mache or plaster of paris if you prefer. Glue these on and paint over the entire ceiling. Textured ceilings can also be simulated by crumbling up kraft paper or aluminum foil which is then flattened out, glued to the ceiling and painted over. If you have any lamps or lights wired to conductive tape under paper or foil, be sure no wires are exposed.

USING YOUR SEWING, NEEDLECRAFT AND OTHER CREATIVE TALENTS IN DECORATING

Utilizing your talents and skills in decorating your dollhouse makes it uniquely your own. If you knit or crochet, you can make tiny blankets or bedspreads, or filet crochet edgings on towels. You can crochet doilies, tablecloths and filet crochet curtains. Cross-stitch and needlepoint artisans can produce wall hangings, rugs and upholstery. If you sew, you can buy small amounts of fabric and make linens, curtains, even rugs for your dollhouse. Using your skills in miniature is a very rewarding and very quick way to decorate.

Knitters and crocheters will find that any design for a full-size bedspread, tablecloth or curtains can be converted to dollhouse size by using very fine thread and very small needles or hooks. Use tiny knitting needles (size 0 or 1) or steel crochet hooks, and the finest yarn or crochet cotton. Some miniaturists actually make their own needles and hooks out of fine wire in order to get the infinitesimal gauge they desire. Often you can separate the strands of fingering weight yarns or embroidery floss and get even finer yarn to work with. Experiment with various stitches, yarns and threads until you get the same number of stitches in 1" as the original pattern got in 12". Or you can adapt a stitch. Even simple stitches like garter stitch will make lovely rugs and bedspreads, but you might want to try granny squares or filet crochet. Working in a finer gauge than you are accustomed to gives you a different perspective and can make an old skill seem new.

There are many kits available for petitpoint or needlepoint rugs, wallhangings and embroidered samplers. Or you can design your own by adapting parts of an existing design. A small accent motif on a large needlepoint canvas may be perfect as the center motif of a needlepoint rug in your dollhouse. Miniature work is difficult because of the size of the materials used, but it is quickly done because the finished piece is so small.

There are many items you can sew for your dollhouse. Some dollhouse wallpaper companies sell accompanying fabrics to match their wallpaper. You can also take a piece of wallpaper to your fabric store and buy solid fabric to match your wallpaper. You can make tablecloths to match or coordinate with the wallpaper in the kitchen and dining room or make drapes in the living room.

■ Tablecloths can be cut from fabric to the size of the table, plus 1-1/2" overhang on all sides. Hem the edges by folding 1/4" to the inside, then fold again. Hemstitch all around.

■ Towels are easily made from pieces of velour or terrycloth. Cut out pieces 3-1/2" x 7" for a towel and 2" x 2-1/2" for a washcloth. Hem the raw edges and fold as desired. Press the folds down.

■ Shower curtains can be made from no more than 1/8 of a yard of fabric. Cut to fit, allowing 1-1/2 times the width of the area to be enclosed. Hem the raw edges. Small pieces of lace can be sewn along the edges for a fancier look. Small metal rings used for jewelry making can be purchased in craft stores and inserted at the top, or the top can be hemmed and a dowel pushed through the hem.

■ Most inexpensive dollhouse beds come with small print bedspreads which can easily be replaced with pieces of coordinated fabric. To do this, carefully remove the original fabric. Draw its outline on a piece of tracing paper. Then cut out a piece of coordinated fabric, allowing 1/8" around all edges for a rolled hem. To roll the hem, roll the edges of the fabric between your fingers to the wrong side of the fabric so that the raw edge doesn't show. With matching thread, tack the rolled edge to the wrong side.

■ Pillow bolsters are made with pieces of fabric cut to the width of the bed plus about 3" overhang on each side, and about 4" long. Hem the longer edges. Insert a small flat piece of fiberfill the width of the bed and about 1" wide in the center of the fabric and fold the fabric over the fiberfill. Fold the exposed edge to the inside and sew in place. Sew through all thicknesses at the ends of the fiberfill.

■ Little pillows can be made by cutting out two squares. With right sides together, sew around three edges. Turn right side out and fill with fiberfill. Sew the last side together, carefully turning in the raw edges.

■ You can make lace curtains and edging by using purchased

With the cast-off projects that didn't really work, you can even create a miniature attic.

rickrack from your fabric store. Rickrack and lace come on bolts in varying widths and types. Some of it looks hand-made. You can use it for valances or curtains, bedspreads or edges. To keep the cut edges from raveling, sew several rows of zigzag stitch along the edges and fold these edges into the hems. Often the top of the rickrack has eyelets through which you may place a dowel for a curtain rod.

Patterns have been developed for window treatments, including cafe curtains, pleated drapes, sheers, tie-backs, balloon shades, swag draperies, cornices and stationary roller shades. These patterns are available in fabric

stores or through your dollhouse dealer. Some include actual pattern pieces; others include charts to help you determine how much fabric you need to fit your situation. Other fabric accessories you can make using these instructions include crib mattresses and bumpers, skirted tables, hassocks, comforters, dust ruffles, pillows, chair cushions, braided rugs, samplers, needlepoint pillows and quilts. The directions given are so complete, you may need no other inspiration for your imagination to develop its own ideas.

If the overwhelming selection of these accessories is not enough for you, you can pur-

A handmade quilt is a charming touch.

chase modeling material and make your own. This material is available in many colors, in kits or separate quantities. It is modeled by hand or with use of special modeling tools and then baked to harden. Before this material is baked it can be reworked until you get it right. The final results can also be painted, decorated, then varnished in glossy or matte finishes. Even a child, and sometimes especially a child, can make beautiful accessories for the house.

CUSTOM DECORATING

If you don't feel creative enough to make your own fabric, knitted or crocheted accessories, you can have pieces specially made for you by the same company that makes the wallpaper. Furniture can be upholstered in coordinated fabric with matching piping. All styles of upholstered furniture from the most traditional to the most modern are available by special order through your dollhouse dealer. Matching fabric window treatments are also available by special order. Pile rugs are also available in many shapes, sizes and styles to match the wallpaper.

WINDOW TREATMENTS

In addition to the window treatments which you can make yourself or have made especially for you, there are many curtain styles that are made in most colors for standard windows. Sheer curtains, balloon shades and cafe curtains are just a few examples of what is available. Drapery and curtain rods as well as shower rods come in many different

styles in brass, chrome or wood finishes. If you prefer matchstick blinds or wooden venetian blinds, you can order these for standard size windows. You can even buy plastic strips for blinds and make your own. Wooden cornices come in different styles

and sizes. They can be painted or covered in fabric to match your drapes or wallpaper.

Window treatments are interesting and diverse: wooden blinds, valences, and shades.

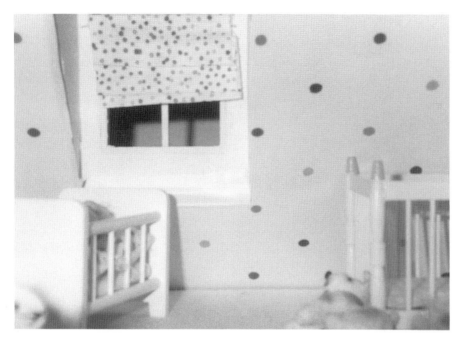

Windows themselves can be decorated by replacing clear panes with stained glass panels, frosted or translucent glass, or acrylic panels. Window mullions can be added to plain windows and "wrought iron" decorative bars can be placed on the outside of windows. Decorative molding can be added around the inside of windows to further enhance their style.

FLOORING AND WOODWORK

Woodwork and wood trim have two main functions in a dollhouse: to enhance the beauty of the interior and to hide the defects. Basically there are two kinds of woodwork—that which goes on the floor and that which goes on the wall. They are usually stained or painted to match, so your choice of one will affect the others.

FLOORING

You may wonder why you need to put wood flooring in a dollhouse since the floors are already wooden. The answer is that you don't have to. You can stain them as is and have perfectly acceptable floors. You can also draw "plank" floors, using a ruler and pencil. Draw lines on the floors of standard or random widths, and at unequal intervals draw the joining places. Before you go to a lot of trouble drawing on floors, be sure that your stain will not erase your drawing. Use a hard lead pencil or trace over your lines, using a fine ballpoint pen and test it on a small surface. It's best to hone your style on a scrap piece of wood anyway.

To imitate Colonial floors,

you can draw nails at both edges of juncture. You can also poke small holes in the floor and stick in toothpicks. Sand the toothpicks even with the floor and you have pegged floors. This can be done on the original floor of the dollhouse or on any of the flooring options described below.

If you do decide to put in wood floors, you have a number of options to consider. The first decision is whether to apply the flooring directly to the floors of the dollhouse or to make the floors removable. To make the floors removable, cut out pieces of mat board to fit in each room and install the flooring on them. If you ever want to change the flooring, you can remove the sheet. If it is necessary to do repairs to any electrical wiring under the floors, movable floors are handy. It is also easier to work on sheets of mat board outside of the house than to work inside the house. One disadvantage is that the edge of the mat board will show on the facing edge of the dollhouse. If you keep all the wiring off the floor, installing flooring direct to the floor is not a problem. You may also feel that floors are permanent, and that you can restain or paint or even make a new dollhouse if you must experiment.

Once you've decided how you are going to install the floors, you have to decide what you are going to install. One option is to use wood veneer which has been laminated onto a paper backing. These sheets are very thin and can be cut to fit with scissors. The sheets can be stained before they are installed. They need to be sanded between coats with a very fine sandpaper. Be sure the surface to be covered is absolutely clean and has been sanded, as the least little speck will cause a bump in this thin material.

All wood flooring should be installed with the length of the flooring parallel to the opening edge of the dollhouse. Of course, this rule can be broken, but one clean line of flooring will look better than multiple ends showing on a facing edge. To install, you can use a spray adhesive, contact cement or high-quality glue. Whatever adhesive you use, you must put a heavy weight on top until the flooring is dry, as it is likely to

Sanding wood floors creates a smooth, finished look.

pop up unless weighted down. This kind of flooring is very thin and uses very little wood. Therefore, some of the more expensive varieties of wood, such as red oak, black walnut and parquet, are available at a much lower cost than the comparable plank or parquet blocks would cost. The wood on these sheets may appear as random plank widths or as all one width. Other options are elaborate parquet, herringbone and checkerboard designs.

Another variety of wood flooring comes in sheets similar to sheets of siding. These sheets are solid wood 1/16" thick which have been scored into 1/4" "planks." They are usually made of pine or basswood and are easy to cut with a razor knife. Unlike real wood or veneer floors, the grain doesn't change on every plank, but crosses the planks over the entire sheet. Also the simulated planks do not have the

Flooring is available in a variety of finishes, or you can stain your own.

normal joints between the planks. With a straightedge and razor knife, you can score across the planks randomly to simulate these joints, however. Since stain may highlight the grain, you may want to distress the wood first, then stain it a dark shade to hide the uniform grain. To distress the wood, take a small pointed object or a pen point and make small indentations and scratches on the wood. Practice on a piece before you install any. These sheets of wood are applied using glue in the same way that you installed siding.

The most realistic and expensive wood floor is made of wood planks or parquet. It comes in a variety of woods, including basswood, pine, red oak, mahogany, cherry and walnut. When choosing a wood, remember that hardwood is more expensive and harder to cut. Other wood in the house, such as the doors and molding, will probably have to be stained to match it to give your house unity. Less expensive wood can be stained to simulate the hardwoods, but you may feel that if you are going to all the trouble of installing wood floors, only the real thing will do.

Planks come in varying lengths, widths and thicknesses. The easiest thickness to saw is 1/16". While planks also come in different widths, the easiest to deal with is 1/2". This is the equivalent of a 6" plank in a house, which is fine for a country house. For random width flooring, you should use 1/4", 1/2", 3/4" and 1" pieces. Most wood planks come in 24" lengths which you will cut to fit your floor. Parquet squares come in

Top: Installing parquet floors is a rewarding project.
Bottom: Plank flooring is an attractive alternative.

different diameters and can be laid by themselves or bordered by planks. They are applied in the same way as planks.

It is easiest to lay flooring across a wide expanse, so you may want to install your flooring before you set in your interior walls. The top edge of the walls will have to be trimmed later, but there will be far less work in-

stalling the floors. (Don't trim an edge where there is a door opening or you will then have to enlarge the opening.) Long planks can be scored with a razor knife across the plank to simulate joints, or you can cut a few planks into random lengths and begin with a short piece, then lay a long plank and cut a short piece to fit. To be sure that your

A room after the floors are laid and before interior trim is installed.

joints fall randomly across the floor, begin each new section with a different length piece.

Installing plank flooring. Make sure the surface is clean and sand away any paint or glue gobs from construction. Lay the planks lengthwise across the opened edge of the house, cutting pieces to fit. If necessary, and it probably will be, sand the edges of the planks to make a smooth joint. After you have a few inches fitted widthwise, push the pieces to the back of the room. Apply a line of glue on the first plank and set in place. After a few seconds, lift the plank to stretch the adhesive and reset. Install the joining piece and continue in this way until all your precut pieces are set in place. Cut more pieces until you have gone about halfway into the room. At this point, check to see if your planks will evenly fit to the back of the room. If there is only a small area uncovered at the back wall, space the last half of the planks slightly apart to compensate. You will probably be putting on floor molding which will cover 1/8" at the wall

anyway, so the wood doesn't have to butt exactly against the wall. Then finish gluing the flooring the rest of the way.

After the wood is installed, you will find that little globs of glue have worked their way to the surface in spite of your best efforts. Use paint thinner on a rag to rub away as much as you can, then sand the surface with fine sandpaper. This glue will act as a sealer and will prevent the wood from accepting stain, so be careful. Be sure to wipe away dust with a damp cloth, even if you don't see any. Stain the wood the desired color. Repeat sanding and staining until you have achieved the desired color, then varnish. Sand between coats. This is a tedious job because it must be done over a period of days to allow the repeated coats to dry, but it will pay off in beautiful floors.

Other flooring finishes are also available. Ceramic tile comes in a multitude of colors, sizes and combinations, available in sheets with "grout" between the tiles. You can lay this tile on any surface using double-faced

tape. Where two sheets join, imitate the grout by drawing or painting a line in the same color as the grout on the surface you are covering and butt the sheets together. This tile can also be used on walls, counter tops and any other surface. Bricks come in sheets or individual pieces and their application on the interior is the same as on exterior surfaces. Bricks can also be used on walls or to cover fireplaces.

WOODWORK AND TRIM

Included in this heading are all of the interior doors, door and window trim, staircases and moldings: baseboard, chair rail and crown moldings, to name a few. While none of these are included in a basic kit (except for staircases), no home is complete without at least some of them.

DOORS

No matter how fancy the interior

Doors can be constructed in a variety of styles.

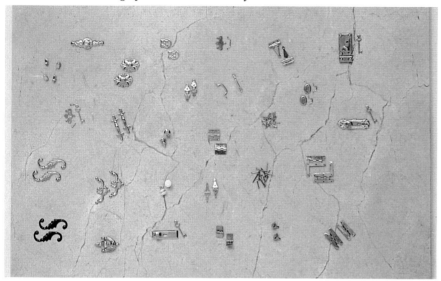

decoration of a house, it is jarringly incomplete without interior doors. There are no real houses without interior doors, yet many "finished" dollhouses omit them. Not only do doors add realism, they hide untold numbers of defects. Electrical wiring often uses doorways to go from room to room. One wallpaper pattern ends and another begins at a doorway.

You can install doors between rooms, but you may also want to build closets in rooms and install bifold or louvered doors. Swinging cafe doors might work well between the kitchen and the dining room. For arched open-

ings between rooms, there is also special trim available. You may want to enlarge an opening between rooms and install French double doors.

These doors should be painted or stained to match the woodwork and floors. Staining and finishing should be done before installation. Little brass doorknobs can be glued on to the doors (do this while the doors are flat, before they are hung). Suddenly, you have a miniature house, not a dollhouse! Use rubber cement to install the doors if you think you might ever want to change the decor of a room; otherwise use white or carpenter's glue.

STAIRWAYS

Interior stairs are one of the components that reveal the cost of a kit. Many kits have you make the stairs by gluing the risers on a piece of wood; others include the finished stairs. Some inexpensive kits use a solid piece of wood to suggest a railing. Other kits ask you to insert the balusters of a railing piece by piece into the lower rail and the hand-rail, using a spacer. None of this assembly is difficult, but it is tedious. More expensive kits will be preassembled with more elaborate balusters and newel posts.

You may want to install the less expensive staircases temporarily with rubber cement so that you can replace them later when you win the lottery.

As well as the standard interior stairs, spiral staircases in wood or metal and pull-down attic stairs are available for special uses. Take care with the stairs, because like interior doors, they are one of the eye-catchers in a dollhouse.

One of the hardest painting or staining jobs is the railings on staircases, porches or balconies.

Staircases can become real eye-catchers if they're built with care.

If the pieces are packaged separately, you can glue them on a piece of paper so they stand upright and spray paint them all around. When dry, the glue can be sanded off the end and the pieces assembled.

WOOD TRIM

Wood trim is another multipurpose interior decoration. First of all, wood trim convinces us that we are looking at a miniature house rather than a toy, because no room in a full-scale house is without trim of some sort. Wood trim in both kinds of houses serves three purposes: it covers the joints between surfaces, it allows us to be a little less careful about their application, and it adds to the style of the house. Trim is easy to apply because it can be stained or painted outside of the house, then glued in place. Use full-length pieces of trim along any one wall. If you want to be extra careful, you can miter the ends so they fit at the corners or you can butt the side pieces against the back piece.

Wood molding is used on the baseboard, at ceiling level, on the walls and around doors and windows. Baseboard moldings come in different styles, including some with shoe molding, some fancy, some plain. Crown and cornice molding are appro-

Trim, such as cornices and turned posts, gives a room a distinctive style.

priate for formal houses, but all houses can benefit from some ceiling treatment, because the joining of ceiling to wall will almost always look a little messy. In a real house, that juncture will have been drywalled smoothly or trimmed in molding and it should also be trimmed in a dollhouse. If you prefer a less formal molding than crown molding, you can use quarter round or cove molding. If you have applied wainscotting or other panelling in your house, you may apply special wainscot trim to make a smooth transition from the top of the panels to the upper wall.

One option which may be appropriate in your house is chair rail, which is a piece of molding placed about 3" above the floor. It frequently separates two different wall treatments—paint and wallpaper, for example. Chair rail was originally used in Colonial days to protect the wallpaper from the backs of chairs. In modern homes it is used primarily for decoration, usually in kitchens and dining

A chair rail—a strip of wood that encircles the room at chair-back level—is an intriguing addition.

rooms. Frequently, wallpaper is used above the chair rail and paint or wainscotting is used below. Of course, personal preference will determine how you do it. In any case, glue the chair rail over the juncture of the two finishes.

Some windows come prebuilt with exterior and interior trim. The inside trim and exterior window snap into the opening and is complete. In other cases, you will have to cut interior trim for each window. Since most windows are a standard size, this isn't too difficult, but it is tedious. You will also have to trim one side of all interior doors.

SPECIALTY DOLLHOUSE DECORATING

Some dollhouses have been especially designed as shops. Often these are single rooms with large windows for display. Others include a shop on the lower level and living quarters on the second floor. Some of these kits even come with shelves, counters, ladders, cracker barrels and other general store necessities. The most common use of these stores is to make a general store or a toy store because of the abundance of accessories available.

You might consider making a store to reflect your own busi-

Specialty decorating allows your fantasy free rein. With the proper accessories, a room or shadow box can become anything from a schoolroom (opposite page) to a general store (left) to a Santa's workshop (below).

ness. For instance, one miniature light wholesaler has decorated a store as a lamp store. Other ideas for shops are a produce market, a bakery, a hardware store, a barber shop, a plant store, a sewing and craft shop, a pet store, a clock shop or a doctor's office. Other uses may take a bit more imagination. I've even heard of one store decorated as a brothel.

DOLLHOUSE PEOPLE AND PETS

Now that your house is decorated, it's time for the people to move in. Dollhouse people can be some of the more expensive items in a dollhouse. They really should be poseable, which is to say their limbs must be bendable so they can use the furniture in the house. Most dolls have wrapped bodies over wires. In some cases their heads are made of fabric, vinyl or porcelain. Their cost depends on the quality of their clothes and accessories and the detail of the painted faces. They are available in all the standard skin tones in a variety of adult and child sizes. They are dressed to fit the time period of the house they are to live in, whether Victorian or modern.

You can also buy specialty figures such as nurses and doctors, bakers, brides and grooms.

Pets can be purchased as porcelain figures or more realistic bendable figures with fur. Bird cages in a variety of colors and styles can be placed in almost every room. Some pets come complete with trouble. For example, you can buy a small porcelain cat caught in the act of spilling a bucket of milk. You might prefer your pets to stay outside. In that case, you can have a rabbit hutch, a dog house or even a stable or barn outside. If you're not careful, you could turn your house into a 40-acre farm.

IN CONCLUSION

One of the best things about the hobby of dollhouse building and miniatures in general is that it is a hobby that never ends. No dollhouse is ever complete or impossible to improve upon. Looking for new pieces and new ideas is something you can do for the rest of your life. So many different skills and talents can be used in the dollhouse that it is a continual challenge and stimulant to our imagination and our abilities. Dollhouses are one of the few hobbies that appeal equally to children and adults and are as enjoyable when being worked on or displayed. Dollhouses, like children, grow on you as well as with you, and will be cherished forever by you, your children and your grandchildren. You will be creating not only a little piece of art, but also part of your personal and family history.

Dollhouse people and pets can provide the final lifelike addition to your dollhouse.

Decorating dollhouses is a hobby that never ends.

·5·

EXTERIOR DECORATING

After you have assembled the house, you can simply paint the exterior walls and roof appropriate colors and be done with it. Or you can choose from siding, brick, stone or even stucco finishes. You can shingle in wood, asphalt or tile. Anything that can be done to a real house can be done in miniature.

In most kits, you will be instructed to wait to install trim, windows, doors and maybe porches until after you have painted or applied exterior finishes. The instructions may also suggest painting these parts separately rather than trying to paint them after they are attached. The people who wrote these instructions have already done things the hard way and probably know what they are talking about; you should probably take their advice about this.

There are ways to duplicate any exterior finish used on a real house. Some finishes imitate the real materials and others actual-ly use them. This chapter will discuss the various finishing methods and the many accessories and extras which can be added to the shell. One of the little bonuses of making a dollhouse is the increase in your vocabulary as you learn about pediments, lintels, medallions, spindles, risers and stringers, dentil molding, corbel brackets, mullions and hundreds of other architectural terms. All of these elements can add to the verisimilitude of your house and also make you more aware of the architectural flavor of your own home and neighborhood.

PAINT

In almost every case, you will paint. Maybe only the trim, maybe only as a background color, but you will paint. So you must decide upon the kind and the color. Some books and instructions recommend semigloss, most recommend flat paint, and all recommend latex paint. There are many reasons for this. First, latex paint washes out of your brushes and off working surfaces easily. Second, latex paint dries very quickly while oil-based paint may take days before it is completely dry. Third, latex paint is cheaper.

There are some health and safety factors to consider in choosing paint. Mercury is sometimes used in paint as a preservative. Although lead is not used in most interior paint today, some exterior paint does contain it and should not be used on a dollhouse. Check the labels and ask the paint salesperson. As this house will probably be used by children, even a small amount of mercury or lead could be dangerous.

In choosing the color paint you need, you have to consider your roof. If you shingle, you may want to leave the shingles their natural color. If not, you can stain, dye or paint them. A natural-looking wood shingle roof makes a statement about the architectural style of the house, and the rest of the outside has to reflect that statement. You shouldn't have an informal roof on a formal house.

At the very beginning of this dollhouse escapade, you made a decision about the architectural style of the house when you chose the kit you assembled. Now, you have to carry through on that decision and either reproduce an actual architectural style in the painting and trim or give your fantasy free rein. For example, a Southern plantation house will probably be painted white, with perhaps only the door painted to complement the color of the roof, while a contemporary house may be stained in natural wood colors. A Victorian house with a lot of gingerbread trim may be painted in five or more colors.

For a truly professional job, some dollhouse manufacturers suggest using a shellac-based primer, then semi-gloss latex enamel. Other manufacturers recommend using only flat paint, as semi-gloss may look sticky. Some say a primer isn't necessary; just use more coats of the same paint. None recommend exterior paint, because it may not dry properly, and none recommend oil-base paints. In the interest of science and because I didn't read the labels, I've used all of them and there's no doubt that latex works best. A flat or semi-gloss finish is a question of taste. The easiest way to go is a good flat interior latex paint. The other options may be somewhat harder to deal with, but may ultimately give you the look you want. You pay your money and take your choice.

The best way to choose your paint colors is to observe the color of houses you pass as you drive around. If you are trying to duplicate a historical period, you may want to go to the library and research the colors used in that time. My general rule is that most houses look best painted in three related colors. One option is to use the darkest shade for the roof and shutters, a medium shade for the main part of the house and the lightest shade for the window and door trim. Of course, you can juggle this combination any way you want, or you can use more or fewer colors. After all, it's your house and you don't have to worry about the neighbors.

Once you've decided on the general color family you want, go to a paint store and look at the paint chip strips, each of which has five to eight colors. Usually there will be a very dark shade, some medium shades and some light shades of the same color. Someone who went to school to study color worked out these combinations and there is a wonderful chance that these colors will look great together. If money is no object, you can get them specially mixed for you, but you will be required to buy at least a quart of each shade— probably a gallon. Since you need no more than one quart for the main part of the house and a pint for secondary colors, you may feel like this is a little excessive. However, you can frequently buy paint on sale and may find that it is cheaper to buy full gallons on sale than quarts that aren't. You can also buy specialty paints in hobby stores in

much smaller quantities but not for much less money.

If you really want to feel clever and economical, put on your jeans and go to the paint store prepared for some heavy work. In most paint stores, there will be a corner filled with mismixed paint. The shopkeepers will be very happy to let you dig through these cans to find colors you want. No one else will buy this paint, since each can is a one-of-a-kind color. You will probably be able to buy a gallon of high-quality paint for less than five dollars and a quart of paint for one dollar. Even if you can't find three colors that match, you can buy one or two and then have the others mixed specially for you.

I've found that store owners are so happy to get rid of this paint, a reminder of their mistakes, that they don't mind your temporarily destroying the back corner of their store. The last time I chose paint, I had a choice of four stacks of gallon and quart cans. Each stack had at least 40 cans. After about an hour of heavy work—lifting, stacking and unstacking—I had spread on the floor of the store about 30 cans of possible colors to paint three dollhouses. The manager insisted on putting the cans away himself, I paid 20 dollars for about 15 cans of paint, and we were all happy.

Probably you will get a better reception during the week rather than on a Saturday afternoon. It wouldn't hurt to call ahead and get the manager to agree to your plan and to find out if they have a large selection or if they have just had a sidewalk sale and gotten rid of it all. The manager will want you to come in and buy the paint even if you make a mess, while the store clerks will only see the mess.

Once you choose your colors, always paint the main color first. Paint or stain the doors and windows and trim before you install them to keep drips and touch-ups to a minimum. Don't think that you won't have to touch up though because no matter how careful you are, paint always manages to travel, splatter and drip. Just wipe it off while it is wet, sand the residual glop and paint over after it is dry. It's best to let each color dry before you paint the next color, but that calls for patience and you may have used yours all up by this point.

When buying paint brushes or using old ones, try to choose good quality brushes that won't leave bristles or old crud from the last paint job in the fresh coat of paint. Remember that every flaw or hair is magnified 12 times on a dollhouse. You will need a 2" brush and various small brushes to paint and touch up details. One invaluable tool is a small edge roller to paint the large areas. These are inexpensive and can be thrown away when you are finished.

Look through your freezer storage containers for a flat dish with a tight cover, big enough to dip your edge roller in. If you do buy large quantities of paint, pour small amounts in this dish. This serves two purposes. The first is that you will keep your paint clean as you work, and you can toss the dregs each day, start-ing fresh the next time. The second is that when some "helper" comes by and knocks over your paint, there will be far less mess to clean up.

Make sure you put the lid back on the large can tightly each time. The temptation is to tap it on lightly in case you need to open it again. Then you put the can on the floor to get it out of the way. Then you kick the can as you walk around the doll-house to paint under the eaves. Then you spend the rest of the day cleaning up. Or you forget you only tapped the lid on lightly and you put the can away. Six months later, when you need to touch up the spot where your niece drew on the siding, you find the paint has dried up.

SANDING

No matter what your final finish is, you will have to sand some, and probably all, parts of your house. I admit that I hate sand-ing and don't do enough of it, but sanding is a necessary evil. If you want to avoid excessive sand-ing, you must be obsessively neat and refuse to glue until you are absolutely sure of the final posi-tion of the pieces. You must sand off all excessive glue. Some glue isn't noticeable until after you paint. Then you will see raised globs which must be sanded off.

You must sand every part before you finish it and you must sand between coats. There are many sanding tools suitable for miniature work. Sanding blocks come in various sizes and can be used to sand large flat areas with-out sanding your knuckles at the same time. Sanding sticks are pencil-sized tools with two flat sides covered with fine sandpa-per; they allow you to get into corners and hard-to-reach areas. You can also buy sanding sponges which bend around cor-ners and work great for columns and trim. You need a variety of sanding materials from paper to sticks, with a variety of textures from medium to the very finest silicone papers. Using the wrong grade paper can make an easy job tediously long or destroy a fine detail. Buy a variety pack of finishing sandpaper first, see what type you use most often, and buy more of it.

One tool I find essential is a trimming plane. It has taken the drudgery out of many a fit-ting job. A trimming plane is only about 3" long and 1-1/2" wide—small enough to fit in most areas. You can find them in most regular hardware stores. Sometimes, no matter how carefully you measure, pieces won't fit. You can sand a protruding edge forever until it goes away or you can plane off the obvious section and sand to exact measurements. A trim-ming plane also easily knocks off rough edges around win-dows and door openings and makes short work of long jobs. Of course, too much planing can make pieces too small, so use it carefully and sparingly.

FINISHING COMPONENTS AND FINISHING KITS

All finishing parts such as shin-gles, siding, extra windows or trim can be purchased separate-ly, but some manufacturers are now providing finishing kits spe-cially made for specific models of dollhouses, which cost only slightly more than buying the parts separately. The advantage of these kits is that the pieces have been precut to fit the exact measurement of the walls and already have wall and door openings cut out. This makes them extremely easy to use. There is no waste, but of course there are no extra parts for mistakes, either. The other disadvantage is that you have no choice as to the shape of the shingles or the type of clapboard included in these kits, but installation is so easy that you may not care.

CLAPBOARD SIDING

Whether or not to apply siding is one of the great watersheds of dollhouse building. If you have built a dollhouse half-heartedly because someone made you— for instance, that cute kid who lives with you—you will probably be able to use your persuasive talents to talk yourself out of doing more than painting the outside. Paint is perfectly acceptable, but the house will always look like a dollhouse rather than a miniature house because real houses have some

kind of texture on their exteriors. Siding and bricks are the two most common finishes.

Clapboard siding comes in either sheets, multiple planks or single planks in many different styles: beaded clapboard, bead and board, and board and batten, for example. With any kind of siding, be sure that the pieces are long enough to fit across the longest unbroken stretch of any wall so that you don't have to make joints halfway across. This is especially true with sheets of siding, as the goal is to make the

Painted trim individualizes a dollhouse kit.

sheets look like single planks and a line between sections will look very obvious. Some siding has tongue-and-groove edges so that one piece laps over the next.

Other siding is shaped to look like it overlaps but actually butts up to the previous piece.

All types of siding are applied in the same way, that is, with a non-water-based glue. Apply a line of glue all around the outside edges of the piece. For a wide piece, also make diagonal lines from corner to corner to provide complete coverage when the piece is placed on the house. Turn the house so that the wall to be covered is horizontal and place the first piece at the lower edge. Move the piece around a little and lift it once to stretch the glue, then replace it. Apply the next piece above the first, continuing to the top. If it is necessary to cut the siding, use a razor knife for thin sheets or a small saw for larger ones. Some kits come with trim which hides

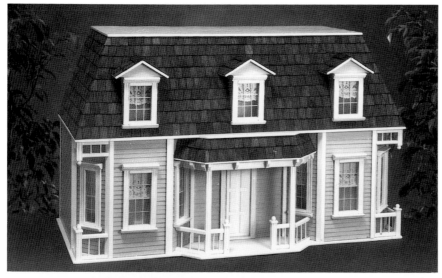

The same house with clapboard siding and with brick.

97

the ends of the siding so that it is not as important to have all pieces cut exactly. If the end of your plank or siding sheet doesn't fit exactly, wood fill can be used to fill in small gaps and sanded before painting.

Because most siding is very thin, it will tend to buckle if it is not securely glued with a strong non-water-based glue. Water-based glue such as carpenter glue is too wet and will warp the wood. Using too little glue can also cause the siding to partially pop off the wall and look wavy and uneven, so be sure that each piece of siding is secure before you apply the next one and that each piece is placed exactly next to the previous one. The siding may look secure until you paint it. Then the water-based paint will cause the siding to buckle unless it is really stuck to the wall. Putting on siding is a relatively fast and satisfying job, and it is easy to do it too fast. Be sure to wipe off any oozing glue before it dries or you will have to

Grout is applied to the laid brickwork.

sand it off before you paint. No matter how careful you are, the siding probably will buckle in one spot. If you don't point it out, no one will notice.

Applying individual beveled planks of siding may sound very tedious, but actually there are certain advantages. The beveled shape makes it unnecessary to lap the boards. Instead, you can butt them up against each other. In most cases, these planks are thicker so there are fewer problems with buckling and gapping. While planks are thicker and thus harder to cut, they are also narrower, so you will probably only have to make straight cuts rather than notches to fit around windows and doors. Whichever kind of siding you choose, you will find that it really finishes the exterior appearance.

BRICKS, BLOCK, SLATE AND STONE

While siding is probably the most common type of exterior finish, anything possible in full-scale is possible in miniature. You may

Excess grout can be wiped off with a rag.

want to use a brick, block, slate or stone finish over the entire house or only in certain areas, but in any case you have two choices in your approach. One is to imitate the look and the other is to duplicate it.

To imitate brick, slate or stone, use a special tape which replicates the mortar between the bricks or stones. First paint a surface the color of mortar, then trim the paper tape to fit the area. Stick the tape to the dry surface. Spread texturing compound on the surface evenly for bricks and with a textured surface for stone. When it is completely dry, remove the backing

tape, which will reveal the mortar-colored paint. You can also use paint instead of texturing compound. Be sure the tape is stuck securely and completely to the dry surface before you paint over it or the paint will seep under, covering the mortar. If this happens, you have uneven looking bricks or slate, which can be touched up and which will look like weathered bricks, if you're lucky.

Larger areas or areas which are very noticeable should be finished with miniature versions of the real thing: brick, slate or stone. You can buy sheets of facing bricks or individual bricks,

After the siding is applied, it can be painted the color of your choice.

but slate and stone come only in individual pieces. These are applied by covering an area with tile mastic or glue, then laying the bricks either in sheets or individually; slate and stone must be laid one by one on the mastic. Corners are tricky, because you must keep in mind that the real materials usually dovetail at a corner. Brick corners make these edges easy to cover, but they are made of plastic and will look a little different than the actual bricks. Be sure to match the color of the brick to the corner brick as closely as possible.

After the bricks or stone are firmly in place and the mastic is dry, use a gray or white grout between the pieces. Grout comes premixed in jars and can be spread directly on the brick or stone and squeezed between them. Wipe off the excess while still wet, then, when it is dry, wipe off thoroughly with a dry cloth. If you don't get all of the grout off, your brick or stone will look older and more weathered. Both looks are appealing and appropriate for different houses.

These natural finishes are ideal for foundations, walkways, chimneys, barbecue pits, garden walls or partial walls on houses. They can be quite expensive to cover large areas or entire houses and their installation can also be quite time-consuming. However they add immeasurably to the realistic look of a house.

STUCCO AND CEMENT
Texture paint products are also available to give the appearance of stucco or cement. These are specially made for miniatures, but you might also try some

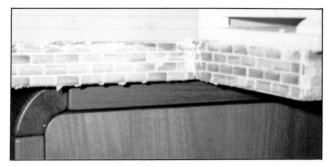

Left: Foundation brick before the grout is cleaned. Below: Brick walkways can be stunning.

products meant for the home on a piece of plywood to see the effect. The powder used to make surfaces non-stick (which is sold in paint stores) can be mixed with paint to make a realistic looking concrete covering on foundations. You may need to paint several coats to get a rough enough surface. You can also mix a handful of sand, real mortar or cement mix into paint to get a rough look.

Some of the most authentic looking finishes are a result of trial and error. Use real houses and architectural styles for your source of inspiration. You will soon find that your eye for detail becomes more developed as you try to duplicate a style in miniature. Experiment on a piece of plywood before you try anything on your house.

As an example of what is possible with a little planning and experimentation, you can reproduce the exterior of an English Tudor style house. First find pictures and photographs of the style house you are trying to emulate. It's important to understand the relationship of the beams and posts to each other on the exterior surface of the house and then imitate them on your house. Draw the positions of the beams and wood trim on the outside surface of the house, keeping in mind the standard size wood strips available in hobby stores. Cover these areas with masking tape. Buy balsa wood trim the desired width or widths and measure and cut out pieces to fit around the house. You may want to distress and weather the beams by scratching and dinging the surfaces with a pencil or pen point, and soften the edges by hitting them with the edge of a pencil or on a table edge. Stain the pieces a dark brown.

With exterior trim, even an English Tudor house is possible.

Stir mortar mix into a light beige, gray or white paint, and paint the exterior of the house between the masking tape strips. You may need several coats to build up the texture on the walls and you may need to experiment with the amount of mortar mix to get the right texture. Since the paint mixture will be fairly thick, you don't have to worry much about the paint seeping over the masking tape. However, you can hold a piece of cardboard along the edge of the tape to keep the edges straight. Since the wood beams and trim on a Tudor house are not all the same size or depth, some of the wood beams should be thicker and thus protrude from the surface, while other pieces will be flush against the surface. You need to keep a photograph of a real Tudor house at hand at all times to use as a guide as to how the wood trim should be arranged. For far less than the cost of siding or brick, you can create an original masterpiece.

SHINGLES

There are almost as many styles of wood shingles or shakes for dollhouses as there are for full-scale houses. Most types of shingles are applied in the same way. You can also buy roof slate, roof tiles and asphalt shingles in sheets similar to the kind used on most modern houses. Some shingles also are made in sheets of pasteboard with the style of shingle drawn on. But the most common type of shingle is the wooden shake made of cedar or other wood. These shingles come in a variety of shapes: fish-scale, rectangular, octagonal,

hexagon, etc. Their size and shape, and the way you finish them, are determined by the style of the house you have built.

Wooden shingles usually come in bags of 1,000—which is enough to do the roof of all but the largest houses. They can be painted, stained or dyed before or after they are applied to the

roof. Shingle dye is an easy way to completely cover all surfaces of the shingle. As shingles are made of very thin wood, if you paint or stain only one side, the untreated side may buckle. Dyeing both sides before they are applied solves that problem.

Balsa-wood half-timbering

103

To dye shingles, you must mix the dye in water and dye handfuls at a time, then spread them out to dry. Drying takes two to three days. This isn't difficult but does take time and can be a bit messy. The finished result is very pleasing. Be sure to follow the directions on the dye and take proper precautions. Wear kitchen rubber gloves, as the thin glove included with most kits will probably tear and your skin will turn shingle brown. If you mix some bleach in water and dip your hands in it, your skin will return to its natural color. However, your fingernails and cuticles will look as if you have done intense gardening for days.

You can make wooden shingles look like slate. Spread the unpainted shingles on newspaper (square-cut shingles work best) and dribble paint in streaks and dots to simulate the uneven appearance of slate. Let dry, then apply the shingles normally to the roof. Paint over the shingles with another coat or two of slate gray paint.

All wooden shingles are applied in the same way. Since they don't have perfectly square edges, before you apply them you will have to paint or stain any area of the roof which shows between the shingles. You may also want to cut strips of copper flashing and glue them to the areas where gables, dormers and chimneys join the roof. Cut the strips about 1/2" wide and glue them to the roof edge to be shingled. Where the shingles do not butt up perfectly against the edge of the protrusion, copper flashing will glint through. This flashing adds an expensive look

Far left: A thatched roof sets off a Tudor-style shop. Below: Regardless of their shape, shingles can be dyed to complement your house and then simply glued in rows to the roof.

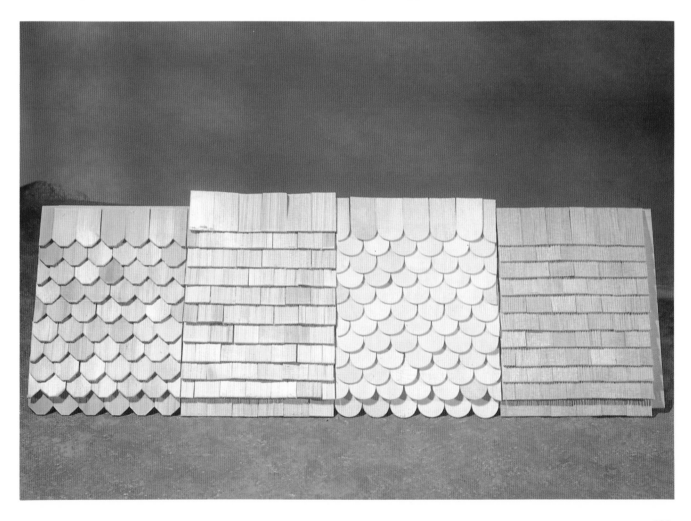

to the roof.

Begin shingling at the lower edge of the roof. Decide if you want the shingles to overlap or butt up to the edge of the roof. Measure and draw a line where the top of the first row of shingles will rest. Draw another line about 1" or the desired distance along the top of the first row of shingles. Then measure additional lines about 1" apart to the roof peak. You can adjust the distance between the rows in order to have a row of full shingles at the peak of the roof, since you will not want to cut or use partial shingles at this visible point.

Using a good glue or panel adhesive (do not use a water-based glue), run a line of glue slightly below the lowest line and begin gluing shingles along the roof edge. As you approach the end of the first row, adjust the distance between the shingles or choose larger or smaller shingles so that you end with a full or half shingle.

On the second row of shingles, begin with a half shingle (cut one with scissors or a razor knife) and end with a half shingle. The object is to stagger the shingles on each row so that a full shingle covers the juncture of two shingles on the previous row. Continue in this way to the peak of the roof. When shingling dormers or porch roofs, you will have to shape the shingles to fit. Along the top of the roof, you may want to lay shingles horizontally across the top or use a piece of ridge molding to trim the top of the roof. Since the shingles are so thin, they can be easily cut or even bent to fit most areas.

In most cases, wooden trim is used to cover some of the edges of the shingled roof. The ridge of the roof is particularly difficult to make look like a real roof. Wooden ridge molding is available and can be painted or dyed to match the shingles or to match other trim on the house. You can use a simple piece that covers the ridge or one with a fancy top trim. Often a thin piece of molding is also used along the side edges of the house to give the roof a more finished look. Thin flat pieces of wood trim, available in most

Shingling cupolas and porches can be tricky.

hobby stores, can be applied to any of the junctures where shingles butt against siding, such as where a porch roof or bay window joins the front of the house, as it is almost impossible to get all the edges of the shingles perfectly even. Wooden gutters can be placed along the long front edge of the house. These gutters are an interesting detail and also cleanly define the edge of the house.

An alternative to wood trim is to place an extra layer of shingles overlapping the areas where shingles join at angles. While this method may look less authentic, it still gives a very pleasing effect. Shingles can be cut with scissors to size and can be laid over the shingles already in place. Wherever a roof turns a corner or changes pitch, such as on a wrap-around porch or on top of a bay window, you will find it practically impossible to match the edges of the shingles perfectly. By using another layer of shingles on top, you give definition and detail to the roof line.

Sheets of copper can also be cut to fit the roofs of cupolas. Trace the shape of the roof on a piece of paper and cut out pieces of copper to match each section of the roof with a little overhang at the lower edge. Glue the pieces of copper directly to the roof, bending the overhang under the roof eave. Cut out smaller strips to lay over the joints. You could also cut one large piece of copper and bend it to fit the roof, smoothing out wrinkles as you go. Be sure to use gloves when handling the copper as fingerprints will tarnish it.

Other alternative roof finish-

Begin shingling at the lower edge of the roof.

es include sheets of corrugated tin for sheds and other style houses. You could even thatch or sod a roof if you really wanted to.

WINDOWS

Most kits come with windows. In fact, one of the main price factors in these kits is whether or not the windows are working or nonworking, and how preassembled the windows are. The less assembled the components, the cheaper the kit. Some kit windows have to be trimmed on the interior with separate pieces of molding, and you may feel that the manufacturer sent you a package of toothpicks instead of window trim or, worse yet, gave you no interior trim at all. Other

windows just pop into the openings, with a fully assembled interior that snaps into place. The advantage of these preassembled windows and doors is that they can be rubber cemented in and easily removed later if you get the urge to repaint or wallpaper. How much and what kind of trim comes with the windows is a very important question and also an expensive one. You either pay for the trim with the window or buy it later.

Just about any first-time builder who makes a collector dollhouse will want working windows. Why? Because they work, they move, they look real, they're wonderful—until they are painted. Then they stick and break.

You will spend a lot of time telling people not to try to open them. Since we are dealing with very thin wood moving in a very small channel, even a very small amount of paint will gum up the works. Many manufacturers suggest using stain on the wood instead to avoid this problem, but even keeping the house in a damp place will cause the wood to swell and make the windows difficult to work.

Another factor is expense. Working windows can cost twice as much as nonworking ones. The fact that many working windows come with interior trim, and most nonworking windows don't, makes up for some of this difference, but maybe not enough for you to make the big leap to working windows throughout the house.

The idea of working windows is so intriguing that you may want to install them anyway, but be forewarned and be careful in how you finish them. One option is to use nonworking windows in most of the house and working windows in a few choice locations, such as in a bay window. Then you can have the thrill of opening windows and the ease and low cost of nonworking windows in the same house.

Besides the windows which are included in kits, there are many optional windows available. These can be used as substitutes for the ones in the kits or they can be added to attics or sidewalls, to bring in light and detail to areas which have no windows. Have you ever noticed how many tract houses have windows only on the front and the back while custom homes and most older houses have windows on all sides? The same is true with dollhouses: the less expensive ones have windows only on the front or back. But you can add them wherever you want.

One of the distinguishing features of new homes today is the use of specialty windows such as Palladian or circlehead styles. You can make your dollhouse distinctive by adding them. Keep in mind the style of the house: a Palladian window might look odd on a farmhouse and a casement window won't do on a Victorian townhouse.

To add a window, draw a template of the window opening on a piece of cardboard by tracing the outside edge of the actual window (not the trimmed edge). With the exterior surface of the window facing you and the interior surface on the cardboard, trace around the outside. Cut this template out and tape it with masking tape to the side of the house. Check its position against the other windows—that is, make sure it is at the same height as the others if it is the same type. Also check its position in relation to the inside of the house. With a pencil, trace around the template and remove it. Check again to see if the proposed window is really in the right position.

Using a razor knife, cut away the siding or other exterior finish. Then, with a small razor saw, cut through the wall of the house. Try to keep the hole the exact size of the template, but remember that you have exterior and interior trim to cover any minor slips. Sand the edges of the opening and square the corners. You are now ready to install the window.

Most windows are installed by inserting the exterior window into the opening. You can use carpenter's glue if you are sure you will never want to remove it to remodel either the exterior

Regardless of the style, period, or color of your dollhouse, there are windows to match it, ready for painting, staining, or personalizing in other ways.

or interior; rubber cement will allow you to change your mind later. Then the windows can be pulled out and you can rewallpaper on the inside or repaint on the outside, painting all the trim separately. The disadvantage of rubber cement is that the windows will not stand up to heavy play without falling out.

Some windows are installed on the surface of the exterior walls. This should be accounted for before you install the siding. Place the window on the wall and trace the edges. Trim the siding so that it will butt up against the window rather than the window fitting over the siding. It's a lot easier to do this before the siding is glued down than after. You probably don't want to install the window before the siding because of the difficulty of painting unless you plan on the window being the same color as the siding. If you install a window after you have already sided, you can try to remove the siding or install over it. Since most siding is uneven, you will have to either add trim to the edge of the window or use wood fill to make the window fit flat.

Working windows

DOORS

Exterior doors come in many styles. I suggest that at first you install the standard doors included in the kit, using rubber cement. Then later, when you become inspired or rich, you can add more elaborate doors with transoms, pediments, stained glass, frosted oval glass inserts, side lights and so on. You install doors in exactly the same way as windows. Remember that exterior doors always open inward.

Adding doors to a sidewall to gain access to a porch or installing French doors and a balcony to an upstairs bedroom are two good examples of places you may want an extra door. Take extra care to get the door exactly even with the interior floor. Cut out the opening for the door, beginning at the lower edge a little above the floor level, then trimming down to floor level. Remember, it's always easier to make a small opening bigger than to make a big opening smaller. Keep the dimensions of any future additions in mind— porches, for example—so that the door is positioned correctly in relation to them.

Installing a window

If you are going to paint a paneled door on one side and stain it on the other, always stain it first, as the stain is likely to seep through the junctures of the panels. After it is dry, you can paint the other side and cover up any stained areas. If you are going to install doorknobs, locks or door knockers, try to do so while the door can be laid flat. Use waterproof cement and try to place the doorknobs at the same height on both sides of the door. Door hardware is one of those important touches that add real interest to a house.

Far left: Adding a window opening.
Left: Adapting a window shape.

One option is to assemble the dollhouse using the exterior doors that come with the kit, then replace them with fancier doors later, when you become inspired or rich.

With extensions, porches, and trim, the same basic kit can take on a dozen different personalities.

Simulated stained glass inserts can add a distinctive touch. Most "glass" that comes in doors and windows is made out of thin sheets of acrylic. Some of these sheets can be removed from the window and replaced by store-bought stained glass inserts, which come in standard sizes to fit most doors, or you can buy sheets of acrylic and cut it yourself to fit your windows. By experimenting with different types of paint or even magic markers, you can stain glass yourself. Charting and art graphic tape, which is available in art supply stores, will simulate the leaded lines in stained glass. This tape comes in varying widths and can be curved gently around sections of color. You can also draw these lines with a fine black pen. If you buy extra acrylic, you can experiment until you get the effect you want.

EXTENSIONS, PORCHES, STEPS, PEDIMENTS, TRIM, MOLDING...

The list of finishing touches available to upgrade the basic kit house is endless. If you look around in a dollhouse store, you will get all kinds of ideas for embellishments. If you have built the shell without too many mistakes, you are probably capable of adding any of these extras, though you may need a good saw to cut through the walls and you will definitely have to measure carefully and follow the directions.

Added rooms on either side change the look completely.

While it may be easier to install every window, door, porch, dormer and extension during initial construction, you may have to get a construction loan to afford it. As with a real house, you may have to live with your dollhouse for a while before you know what you want or feel the need to improve. Cutting extra windows and doors can be done after siding. Shingles can be removed if you decide you want to install a dormer or chimney. It is a good idea to save some paint, along with some original shingles and siding, in case you do decide to remodel later.

Many manufacturers make extension kits which fit onto the side of a house. You can add the extension during initial construction or add it later. Building an extension kit requires the same skill and tools as building the original house. The main difference is that on the extension one sidewall is partially missing. If you use an extension meant to fit a certain model house, the extension's foundation on the open wall will slide under the sidewall of the house. There will also be a flat surface on the open wall to support the second floor and roof during construction and to attach to the rest of the house. Extensions are usually glued and/or nailed to the main house. Be sure the house and the extension are on a flat surface when you join them and that they are held together firmly with clamps or masking tape while the glue is drying.

As you will probably want a door between the extension and the house on all levels, you should cut it out before you permanently attach the extension. Measure carefully before you cut to get the doors and floors to match.

If you add an extension to a house which has some type of exterior finish on it other than paint, you may want to remove this finish, at least where the house and the extension join so that the two parts have flat surfaces to bond together. You can remove siding with a razor knife,

Top: Adding a porch. Bottom: Dormers are eye-catching additions.

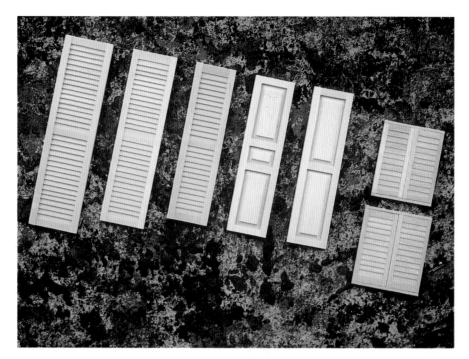

but it isn't easy. It may be easier to cover the whole wall with a thin piece of plywood or other hobby wood, no thicker than 3/16". You will have to replace any corner trim to cover the exterior edge, but you then have a smooth interior wall to decorate and attach the extension to. If you are planning on cutting doors or other openings in the existing wall, cut the wood cover first, then cut through the existing wall to get a perfect match.

You can also try to incorporate the existing exterior finish into the decorating scheme of

Left: Shutters dress up the exterior. Below: A house with added shutters, cupolas, and wrap-around porch.

the new rooms. Existing windows can be enlarged into doors, and siding can be turned into paneling with a little paint. Wood trim and molding will cover the places where the extension and the exterior wall don't quite meet.

Porches are another popular addition to many dollhouses. They are built onto a house in much the same way as an extension—that is, you usually build them separately, slip their foundation under the exterior walls of the house, join the roof to the

Adding a chimney can provide the perfect finishing touch.

side of the house and glue some supporting roof posts to the side of the house. Just as with extensions, it is difficult to get a flat surface to grab onto if you have put siding on the house, but since most of the joining surface is, like the siding, horizontal, it's not as big a problem. Don't be tempted to postpone the siding until after you've put on the porch, because it is far more difficult to put on siding around and under porches than on a flat surface. You can also cleverly figure out where the porch will fit, mark the walls and leave them bare where you will be joining the pieces.

Porches are often made to fit across the front of the house, but often a second porch can be joined to the first to make a wrap-around porch. One of the real tests of a good dollhouse kit manufacturer is how adaptable the separate components are. Can two porches equal one wraparound without requiring much adjustment or additional trim? If a manufacturer makes a gazebo and a porch, can you join the two at the end of the porch to make a really elaborate and attractive addition?

Roof decorations are another way to add interest to a house. While it is easier to add dormers and chimneys before you shingle and, in some cases, before you attach the roof, it's never too late. If you are going to cut through a shingled roof, you should remove the shingles first, at least around the cutting edges, so you know you are cutting correctly.

Dormers can be a little tricky to assemble because they seem to be all angles with no straight edges. Use a lot of masking tape to hold them together during assembly. If walls are to be sided, do that before they are attached. If you know what wallpaper you will be using in the room, wallpaper the interior before the dormer is installed. Shingle the roof after the dormer is joined to the house so that you can cover any uneven edges where you cut through the roof. Neaten up the shingles along the sides.

If you are adding a chimney, it should be attached directly to a smooth, unshingled surface. Shingles can be removed with a razor knife and the glue scraped off. Then the chimney can be glued on. Paint or brick the chimney before you add it to the roof. Replace any broken shingles around the edges and you're done. Weathervanes can easily be attached to any roof because they just pierce the wood and shingles like a nail.

Appropriate exterior trim is usually included in a kit. Federal style window pediments will not be included in a farmhouse, and gingerbread trim will not accompany a mansard roof. You may, however, want to add more trim to jazz up your house, and many types are available. Most good hobby or dollhouse stores will not only have interesting trim and molding, they will also carry very thin, specially shaped wood which may come in handy if you have made a mistake in construction and need to hide something or if you have broken or misplaced pieces of your kit. Sometimes a slightly larger or smaller piece of wood will cover a mistake or make an installation a lot

easier. If you can't get a piece of trim to fit, go to the hobby store and find an alternative piece. Hobby wood can be bought by the single piece or in packs of standard size pieces that can be used in many applications. These packs are available in balsa, which is easy to cut and carve for moldings, and in plywood for sturdier applications. It's better to get a piece of wood to solve your problem than to tear your hair out.

There are certain advantages to using the additions, dormers and porches made by the same manufacturer because these pieces have been designed to fit together. On the other hand, you may find that mixing pieces from different manufacturers can give you a superior finished product because each manufacturer has certain strengths and weaknesses in their designs. For example, you may love the basic style of a house, but hate the cheap gingerbread trim. In that case, scrap the trim and buy trim from another manufacturer. Substitute windows, change staircases—it's up to you. Save the rejected pieces because you may be able to use them somewhere else or in the next house, where they might be more suitable. Nobody said you have to make the exact house shown on the advertising brochure.

LANDSCAPING

No house is an island and no house is really complete without some landscaping. A full-scale, newly built house looks raw and callow without landscaping. A dollhouse, on the other hand, looks okay without landscaping,

but really special with it.

Of course, there may be problems. If you want to be able to view the house from more than one side, you may want to put it on a turntable, making landscaping difficult or impossible unless you turn the entire landscape. A front-opening house is also a little more difficult to landscape as the front wall will always be opening into the front yard. However, landscaping is so terrific that it's worth the extra effort—even if it's only a little grass and a few small plants.

Sometimes the display location of a dollhouse makes it possible to landscape with house plants. If a dollhouse is placed on a table with house plants nearby, the greenery suggests landscaping, even though it's out of proportion to the house. If the dollhouse is part of a room's decorating scheme, house plants may tie the house into the room. The dollhouse may even be used as a base of a table if it has a flat roof.

For more traditional landscaping, the first step is to cut a piece of 1/4" thick plywood to fit the table top where the dollhouse will be displayed. If you plan on placing it on a turntable, you will probably want to round the corners so they do not accidentally gouge walls or people. Paint the plywood black or green. Then cover the lawn surface with a grass mat, available in most hobby stores in different size sheets, using white glue to attach it to the board. This is the simplest landscaping of all. As with a full-scale house, you will probably not be satisfied with just lawn.

Below left: One landscaping option is to surround your dollhouse with ordinary house plants. Below right: Grass matting can simulate a lawn. Bottom and next page: Landscaping can be as elaborate as a formal Tudor garden.

Before you proceed any further, make a sketch of your landscape plan to scale on a large piece of paper. Decide first on the more permanent options, such as walkways, fences and walls, keeping in mind the type of house and whether any walls will be opening into the yard. Then decide on the location of flower beds, bushes and trees. Ground foam comes in a number of colors which duplicate spring grass, flowers, dirt, gravel, etc. It can be applied over the grass mat as desired to make flower beds, pathways or gardens. Apply white glue to the areas where you want the foam

and sprinkle on the appropriate type. Blow the residual foam away. Lichen can also be glued on to make bushes. Brick and stone walls can be added to give definition to the flower beds. You can even use real pebbles or stones if you keep the 1" to 1' proportions in mind.

Along with those little cone-like trees we all remember from train sets, there are also authentic looking trees available in many different sizes. Railroad trees are often not in dollhouse scale, but they can sometimes be used as bushes. You can also use putty powder to make your own tree trunks and use lichen for

leaves if you feel the need to reproduce a favorite apple tree from your childhood. Modeling clay can be used to make tree trunks and even tiny little leaves which can be painted realistically. If you need realistic looking hedges, turf, foliage, rose bushes or loose flowers to plant in the flower beds, they are all available. You might want to buy a Christmas tree which can be planted in the garden when not festooned with lights and decorations inside.

Many companies and independent craftspeople also make potted plants which can be set on the porch, added to flower

boxes or used as hanging baskets. Local miniature shows and shops usually have an assortment of these because craftspeople seem to compete with each other to make the most realistic flowers. If you want to try your hand at making flowers, you can buy kits for practically all types of house plants or you can go to a silk flower supplier and adapt materials to miniature versions.

Even if you don't feel capable of making your own flowers, you may have a talent for combining the tiny treasures you buy into interesting vignettes. Little fruit baskets and bushel baskets, flower pots and window boxes are available in many sizes. You can even buy wicker tape and make your own baskets if you desire.

Other authentic details to consider for your landscaping are trellises for climbing roses and outside planters to decorate yards and foundations. Miniature gardening tools can be left out to authenticate the way an actual yard looks. These tools, planters and trellises can be made out of balsa wood or purchased from accessory suppliers. Complete gardens can be planted and baskets of the newly picked crops can be sitting in the yard, peas waiting to be shelled on the front porch.

Vegetables and fruits are fun to make with modeling clay, especially if you are handy with a paint brush, as the detailed painting is what makes the simple shapes of most food interesting. Simply roll tiny bits of clay into the rough shapes of the vegetables, then use toothpicks and modeling tools to shape tiny apples and oranges, cucumbers and broccoli. This is one of the best projects to do with kids because you can smash your mistakes and start over.

If your house needs city touches, you can buy a fire hydrant, a street lamp post and electric or gas meters. Install a

Landscaping makes a dollhouse look much more like a miniature home.

mail slot and a brass door knocker. For the country look, you might consider a rural mailbox or a picket fence. Many different style fences are available ready-made or can be made from slats of hobby wood. Buy appropriate size strips and lay them out on a table, arranging them until you get the right look. It's good to have photographs of actual fences to use as a guide before you at all times. Use waterproof cement to join the pieces, then attach the posts to the plywood base, using modeling clay or putty to hold them up.

Porch swings, benches and lawn furniture true to every historical period are available. You can have a hot tub or a wishing well, a cast iron park bench or a wicker settee, a gas grill or a camp fire. The dollhouse children probably need a swing set, a wagon, a sled or a bicycle. Anything you can have full size, you can probably get in miniature. Many of these accessories are available in kits, or you can design them yourself, using the many materials available to you.

There are many beautiful outdoor buildings available. Gazebos which fit into porches or which stand separately are made by dollhouse manufacturers. These kits consist of a rounded foundation and a roof supported by posts and railings. The same skills needed to build a house are needed to build a gazebo, including shingling, painting and making railings. If the gazebo is painted to match the house and joined to it by a slate walk, it is a beautiful addition to the landscape.

Greenhouses, either free-standing or attached, are a wonderful way to display the plants you have made. Toolsheds complete with miniature tools are interesting additions to a backyard and are much easier to keep neat than real ones, though you can buy (or make) miniature

Fences and gates can deter miniature intruders.

sawdust and woodcurls for authenticity. Stables can also be made from kits in either two-bay or four-bay models, and simple barns can be made from plans or a kit. There are entire cottage industries which specialize in buildings which are available in kits or are preassembled.

If you have electrified the inside of your house, you can also electrify the outside with porch lights, Christmas lights and post lights. The wires can be hidden underneath the landscaping. The outdoor lights can be put on a separate circuit and a switch, for independent operation, or turned on with the house lights.

Adding landscaping and buildings to your yard is something that grows with you as your own skills develop and as you think of new ways to individualize your miniature world. If you do want to experiment with making a building from scratch, you might as well start small. Here, for example, are instructions for an outhouse. The principles of constructing this outbuilding apply to all small buildings, including doghouses, sheds, stables or any small one-story buildings. Let these instructions be the beginning of many buildings, perhaps some with a less mundane purpose.

OUTHOUSE

Materials:

Base: 1/4" thick balsa wood 3-1/8" x 5"

Door, seat and trim: 1/16" thick balsa wood 3" x 10"

Support strips: 1/4" square strips of balsa wood totaling 48"

Walls: Four 1/16" thick plywood sheets 3" x 9" long

Roof: One 1/16" thick plywood sheet 3" wide and 5" long

Door jambs: 1/4" thick balsa wood 7" long and 3/4" wide

Glue, small pieces of plastic tape, paint, miniature landscaping gravel

Centered on the base, make a 3" square of 1/4" square strips, allowing 1/16" at the front and back for back and front walls. Now for the walls: from the plywood, cut 1 piece 8" tall and 1 piece 9" tall, for the 2 sidewalls.

Cut 2 pieces 8" tall at one side and 9" tall at the other side, for the front and back. On the front, cut out the door opening: 2" by 7", beginning at the narrow straight end. Cut out 3 door jambs of balsa wood 1/4" wide— two 7" long and 2" long. Glue them to the inside of the door opening, overlapping the door opening by 1/8". Glue square strips to long edges of sidewalls, beginning 1/4" from lower edge. Glue back to sidewalls and glue building to base. Cut out 2 strips of balsa wood 1-1/2" wide and

3" long. Notch 1/4" corners on 1 side of each piece and cut out a 1" circle at center of 1 piece. Glue these pieces to the back and sidewalls to form seat and glue on cut out circle for lid as shown in photo. Glue on the front of the building. From plywood, cut out a piece 5" long and center on top of building. From balsa wood, cut out a door 2" by 7" and carve out a small half moon. Cut out a small piece of 1/4" square for doorknob and glue on. Tape small strips of plastic tape across edge of door and

Outbuildings can include gazebos, sheds, barns, or even outhouses.

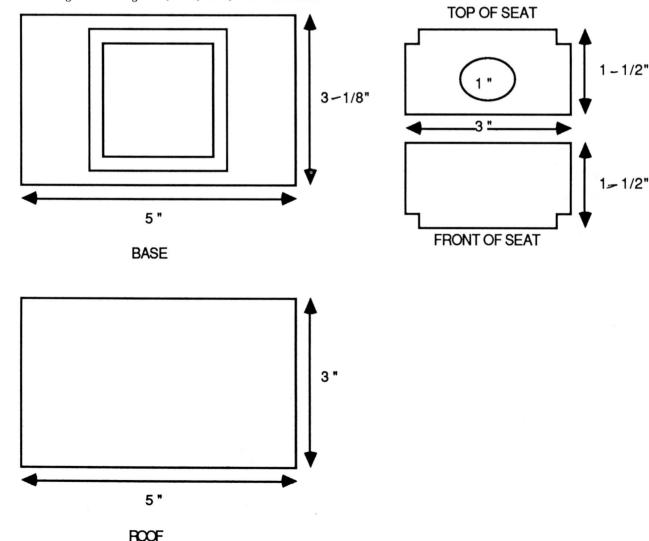

125

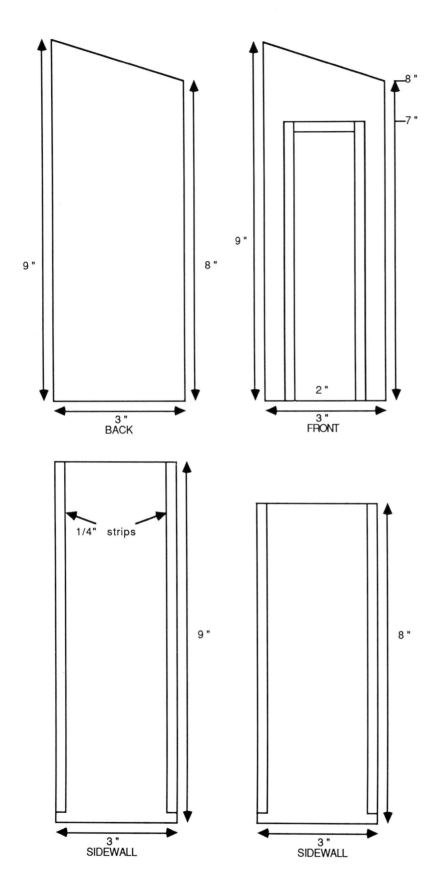

front for hinges.

Paint the house the desired color. To roughen the texture, paint very thickly, deliberately making obvious brush strokes. While the first coat of paint is tacky, dab your finger in a slightly darker shade of paint and smear streaks on the walls.

The roof can be shingled, painted or graveled. To gravel the roof, paint the roof. While still wet, sprinkle fine dirt or landscaping gravel on the wet paint. When dry, apply a second coat of paint.

After writing this chapter, I asked my husband to build another outhouse as a test of my instructions. He ended up building a completely different outhouse, using some of my ideas, but creating and improving as he went along. That is what I hope you will do as you invent, create and build, using some of the ideas and techniques suggested, but also adapting your own ideas to this fascinating hobby. The goal of this book is to introduce you not only to a unique form of recreation, but also to a kind of creation as you build your own miniature world.

Plans for building an outhouse.

CONTRIBUTING SUPPLIERS

We would like to thank the following manufacturers, who generously shared their kits, components, photos, and advice.

DOLLHOUSE KITS AND COMPONENTS

Houseworks
2388 Pleasantdale Road
Atlanta, GA 30340
404-448-6596

Real Good Toys
10 Quarry Hill
Barre, VT 05641
802-479-2217

Walmer Dollhouses
2100 Jefferson Davis Highway
Alexandria, VA 22301
703-548-8804

ELECTRIFICATION KITS AND COMPONENTS

Cir-Kit Concepts, Inc.
407 14th St. N.W.
Rochester, MN 55901
507-288-0860

DOLLHOUSE FURNISHINGS

Aztec Imports, Inc.
6345 Norwalk Road
Medina, OH 44256
216-725-0770

LANDSCAPING MATERIALS

Life-Like Products, Inc.
1600 Union Avenue
Baltimore, MD 21211
301-889-1023

PUBLICATIONS

Nutshell News
Crossroads Circle
P.O. Box 1612
Waukesha, WI 53187
414-796-8776

TOOLS

Excel Hobby Blades Corp.
399 Liberty Street
Little Ferry, NJ 07643
201-807-1772

WALLPAPER

Mini Graphics
2975 Exon Avenue
Cincinnati, OH 45241
513-563-8600

WOODEN MOLDING AND TRIM

Northeastern Scale Models, Inc.
P.O. Box 727
Methuen, MA 01844
508-688-6019

METRIC CHART

INCHES TO CENTIMETERS

INCHES	CM	INCHES	CM
1/8	0.3	19	48.3
1/4	0.6	20	50.8
3/8	1.0	21	53.3
1/2	1.3	22	55.9
5/8	1.6	23	58.4
3/4	1.9	24	61.0
7/8	2.2	25	63.5
1	2.5	26	66.0
1-1/4	3.2	27	68.6
1-1/2	3.8	28	71.1
1-3/4	4.4	29	73.7
2	5.1	30	76.2
2-1/2	6.4	31	78.7
3	7.6	32	81.3
3-1/2	8.9	33	83.8
4	10.2	34	86.4
4-1/2	11.4	35	88.9
5	12.7	36	91.4
6	15.2	37	94.0
7	17.8	38	96.5
8	20.3	39	99.1
9	22.9	40	101.6
10	25.4	41	104.1
11	27.9	42	106.7
12	30.5	43	109.2
13	33.0	44	111.8
14	35.6	45	114.3
15	38.1	46	116.8
16	40.6	47	119.4
17	43.2	48	121.9
18	45.7	49	124.5
		50	127.0

BIBLIOGRAPHY

Drysdale, Rosemary. *Miniature Crocheting and Knitting for Dollhouses.* Dover Publications, 1981.

Jacobs, Flora G. *Doll's Houses in America: Historic Preservation in Miniature.* Washington Doll's House, 1974.

Nutshell News magazine. Kalmbach Miniatures, Inc., 1989-1991.

Porter, Bob. *Building With Bob.* Hobby Book Distributors.

Stephenson, Fred. *The Dollhouse Builder's Handbook.* Design Technics Miniatures, 1989.

Three-in-One Dollhouse Planbook. Houseworks, Inc., Atlanta, GA.

Waldron, Dennis, and Sandy Thomas. *Dollhouses to Dreamhouses.* Greenleaf Products, Inc., 1989.

Worrell, Estelle Ansley. *The Dollhouse Book.* Van Nostrand Reinhold Co., 1964.

INDEX